QUESTIONS & ANSWERS ABOUT

BRITISH
HISTORY

QUESTIONS & ANSWERS ABOUT

BRITISH
HISTORY

MARKS &
SPENCER

Marks and Spencer p.l.c.
PO Box 3339
Chester, CH99 9QS
www.marksandspencer.com

Copyright © Exclusive Editions 2003

Originally created by
Monkey Puzzle Media Ltd

ISBN 1-84461-198-1

Printed in Dubai

Written by Peter Chrisp, A.N. George,
Jason Hook and Paul Mason

Illustrated by Adam Hook, John James,
David McAllister and Michael Posen

Contents

Heroes and Villains

Disaster and disease

Kings and Queens

Crime and Punishment

Explorers and Adventurers

Raiders and Conquerors

Who were the first British settlers?

Over 500,000 years ago, prehistoric humans started to migrate from Europe to Britain. They were hunters who wandered around the land looking for animals like sabre-toothed tigers, oxen and deer. These early people belonged to a species called *Homo erectus* (which means upright human being). You could say they were the first people to conquer Britain.

Who was *Homo sapiens*?

Over 230,000 years ago a new species of human replaced *Homo erectus*. Called *Homo sapiens* (wise human being) they were more intelligent than their predecessors and knew how to build shelters from wood and animal bones. These early humans were very different to us, but we do have something in common with them – we belong to the same species. We are all *Homo sapiens*!

Did the first settlers sail to Britain?

No, they walked! The seas were much lower in prehistoric times, and Britain was not an island. There was no need for the Channel Tunnel as Britain was still connected by land to the European continent.

How was the land conquered?

Around 8500 BC more settlers arrived from Europe. They were farmers who brought with them seeds for growing barley and wheat. They settled mostly in the south and east of England, as well as in Scotland and Ireland. Over the years, they cleared much of Britain's forests. The wild land had been conquered by humans.

Early Britons building huts.

10

Where did the Celts come from?

By 500 BC, fierce, warlike people were finding their way to Britain. They were called Celts, and they came from central Europe. They travelled around the region and gradually became the main race of people in France, Germany, Spain and Britain.

Celts feasting.

How did the Celts change life in Britain?

When the Celts first came to Britain, people lived in small villages surrounded by the fields they farmed. Soon, however, the small villages grew into tribal areas. Each tribe had its own king and queen. Neighbouring tribes made war on each other and there were fierce battles.

What was a druid?

The Celts had priests called druids. They organized religious festivals, during which they cut mistletoe with golden sickles. Some disagreements between tribes of Celts were settled by these mysterious druids. Although they did not take part in battles, they shared in the spoils of war.

How did the Celts bleach their hair?

Many Celts used lime to bleach and stiffen their blonde hair, then combed it back from their foreheads to give it the appearance of a horse's mane. Officers of high rank used to grow big moustaches too. They believed this gave them a dignified appearance.

Why did the Celts smell so good?

The Celts were proud of their cleanliness, and used soaps and perfumes. They were also proud of their appearance: they liked to wear brightly coloured shirts; special trousers known as bracae; and enormous cloaks with checked or stripy designs, draped over their shoulders and fastened with beautiful brooches of gold or silver.

NAKED FURY

The Celts were a frightening sight in battle. They preferred to fight stark naked – except for their favourite golden armlets and a ring around their necks called a torc. Huge horns were played during a fight, and the naked warriors sang songs and screamed to frighten their enemy.

When did the Romans conquer Britain?

In 55 BC, the Roman general Julius Caesar was attempting to conquer France. The British Celts, or Britons, rushed to help their neighbours, and an angry Caesar swore revenge. After France was captured, he turned his attention to Britain, but fierce storms in the English Channel drove the Roman ships away. It was not until AD 43 that the Romans made another serious attempt to conquer Britain. That year 40,000 Roman troops launched a successful invasion, and Britain became Britannia – a Roman colony.

Could anyone become a Roman soldier?

Ancient Rome was a truly multi-cultural society. Anyone from a conquered country could join the army. They could even rise to become emperor – the famous emperor Septimus Severus was Libyan. When foreign soldiers retired from the army, they were given Roman citizenship.

What was life like in Roman Britain?

The Romans built large towns and introduced the lifestyle of their empire. Towns contained a main square where there were shops, workshops, offices and law courts. The square was also used as a market, where Britons could buy things they had never seen before – including onions, olives, grapes and oysters.

How did the Romans roam?

Before the Romans arrived, Britain's only roads were dirt tracks. To make it easier for their army to travel round the country, the Romans built 16, 000 kilometres of excellent roads, wonderfully straight and constructed from three layers of stones and grit. They also built inns and forts where weary travellers could rest for the night and get a bite to eat.

Who was worth their salt?

Sometimes Roman soldiers were given salt as part of their wages. This was known as *salarium*, from which we get the word 'salary'.

Which queen found the Romans taxing?

Although some tribes of Celts co-operated with the Romans, most fought back against the invaders. One tribe called the Iceni was ruled by a famous warrior queen called Boudicca. She led a rebellion against the Romans in AD 60 after they had demanded the Iceni pay heavy taxes. But the rebellion was crushed, and Boudicca killed herself by taking poison.

Who borrowed their gods?

The Romans borrowed many of their gods from the Greeks, but gave them new names. Roman soldiers also worshipped foreign gods they had discovered during campaigns abroad. One of the most popular was the Persian god Mithras.

Why did the Romans leave Britain?

By AD 300, the Roman Empire was so vast it was becoming impossible for the army to patrol all of its borders. Enemies raided Roman settlements throughout north-east Europe. Tribes called Picts and the Scots were overrunning northern Britain, and Saxon marauders attacked from the south. By AD 410 the army was needed to defend Rome, and Britain was left to fend for itself.

HADRIAN BUILDS WONDER WALL

In AD 122, the emperor Hadrian ordered his soldiers to build a massive wall across the north of Britain, to prevent an invasion by barbarian tribes that lived there. Hadrian's Wall took six years to complete and was 117 km long. The ruins of the wondrous wall can still be seen today.

How good was the Roman army?

For hundreds of years, the Roman army was the best in the world. Roman legionaries could march for huge distances, and fought with great discipline. They knew how to build forts and bridges, and construct giant catapults that could hurl enormous boulders.

Roman soldiers on the march.

Roman soldiers building Hadrian's Wall.

Who were the Anglo-Saxons?

The Angles, Saxons and Jutes were European tribes that spoke a German language. They came from territories that are now in Holland, southern Denmark and western Germany. After the Romans left, these tribes made more and more raids on the south coast of Britain. At first, they returned home after each attack, but gradually they decided to settle. The new arrivals mixed together and became known as Anglo-Saxons.

An Anglo-Saxon thane.

Why were the Anglo-Saxons invited?

By AD 430, many Britons were under the rule of a warlord named Prince Vortigern. Facing attack from marauding tribes of Picts and Scots, Vortigern invited Anglo-Saxon warriors to come and fight on his side. There was no problem getting them to come, but more of a problem getting them to leave. They liked the country so much they stayed! These fierce Anglo-Saxons claimed vast areas of land for themselves.

Who were Hengist and Horsa?

In 455, Vortigern's new Anglo-Saxon friends turned on him. He was defeated in battle by the brothers Hengist and Horsa, and an Anglo-Saxon kingdom was established in Kent. By 491 the Anglo-Saxons had control of the south coast, and by 600 they ruled the whole of England.

What does England mean?

The word England comes from an Anglo-Saxon word meaning 'land of the Angles'. This referred to the people called Angles, rather than suggesting that England had funny shaped hills!

Who was the first king of England?

Anglo-Saxon settlements united themselves into seven different kingdoms, called Kent, East Anglia, Sussex, Essex, Wessex, Mercia and Northumbria. The kingdoms were ruled by different leaders who fought to gain control of each others' territories. By 757, King Offa of Mercia had become ruler of all the kingdoms – the first true king of England.

What were churls and thanes?

At the top of Anglo-Saxon society were the thanes, the lords who owned all the land. They rented land to farmers called churls, who had to grow enough to keep their families and pay the thane. Even worse off than the churls were the poor slaves, who depended on their masters for food and lodgings.

King Arthur leads his men into battle.

Did King Arthur really exist?

Nobody knows for sure who inspired the legend of King Arthur. But it may have been Owain Ddantgwyn, a warlord who led the Britons in glorious battles against the Anglo-Saxons. His headquarters were in a disused Roman fort in Wales, called Caerleon. This fort may have inspired the legend of Camelot, where the knights of King Arthur met at a round table.

BEOWULF SLAYS A DRAGON

The early Anglo-Saxons had a rich tradition of story-telling, but they could not write. When they settled in Britain they learnt Latin – and wrote down some of their beautiful stories. One of the most famous is the poem *Beowulf*, the first great work of English literature. It tells of the heroic warrior Beowulf, who fights with monsters and fire-breathing dragons.

Did the Anglo-Saxons have holidays?

People in Anglo-Saxon times celebrated eight major 'holy days', or holidays, every year. They had celebrations for such times as the planting of seeds and midsummer's night. At harvest time, children made corn dollies – a tradition that has lasted to the present day.

How was Yule celebrated?

Yule was a twelve-day celebration during which the Anglo-Saxons burnt a Yule Log in honour of the coming of spring. This custom survived into Christian times, when it became a Christmas tradition. Yule is now another word for Christmas.

Who were the Vikings?

The Vikings were farmers from Sweden, Norway and Denmark, who became known for seafaring and piracy. In summer, while Viking women and older men looked after the farms, the young men set off on their ships to pillage and loot. Their warriors believed that bravery was the greatest talent a man could have. The highest mark of respect in Viking society was having an epic poem written about your brave deeds. Poetry was very important to the Vikings – it was the way they recorded their history.

When did the Vikings conquer Britain?

In 787, three mysterious ships approached the coast of southern England. From them rushed bloodthirsty warriors, who looted and burned coastal settlements then sailed away over the horizon. It was the first of many Viking attacks that terrorized England, and soon the raiders were coming not to raid but to conquer. By 850, the Vikings had built forts down the east coast of Britain from the Orkneys to the Thames. In 865, they attacked and conquered Mercia, East Anglia and parts of Northumbria. The Vikings were here to stay.

Who tried greatly to stop the Viking invasion?

Alfred the Great led Saxon attempts to fight off the Viking invasion. The king himself designed new ships with high sides that could withstand Viking arrows. After Alfred won battles against the Vikings, they retreated into territory north of London – which became known as the Danelaw.

How did Cnut make waves?

By 1016, a wise Viking called Cnut had become the undisputed king of England. He became famous for standing on a beach and ordering the waves to stop advancing. This was not a foolish act of vanity but an attempt by Cnut to show his people that no man is as powerful as God or nature.

What did the Vikings do with dragons?

They carved dragons out of wood, and used them to decorate their ships: a dragon's head at the prow, and a dragon's tail or a smaller head at the stern. The Vikings considered their ships, which they called longships, to be their most important possessions.

A raiding party of Vikings pillage and burn a settlement in England.

A Viking longship.

How did the Vikings build their longships?

A Viking first felled some oak and ash trees and stored the timber in shady woodland to season it. Prayers were said before the ship was built. The finished longship was painted over with a tar made by roasting pine-logs over a slow fire and collecting the resin as it oozed out. Sails were made from striped linen.

VIKINGS SCARED OF GHOSTS

When a Viking died, relatives did not carry the body out through the door. Instead they passed it through a hole in the wall which was immediately closed up again. This was meant to confuse the ghost of the dead person, so it could not find its way back into the house. During a funeral, Vikings disguised themselves by blackening their faces. This way, the ghost of the deceased would not recognize them and decide to haunt their home.

Why was Leif unlucky?

Vikings led by a man called Leif the Lucky managed to sail all the way from their settlement in Greenland to North America. Leif and his people settled on the east coast, but then Leif's luck ran out – Native Americans killed all his people's cattle and they had to sail home to Greenland.

What was at the end of the rainbow?

The Vikings worshipped a number of gods, whose father, or chief god, was Odin. They believed that a rainbow was a bridge that connected earth with the halls of Odin in the sky. If warriors fought bravely, they would be allowed to travel along the rainbow and join their gods for a never-ending feast.

Have you sung a Viking song?

Possibly – many playground songs can be traced back to the Vikings. These include 'In and Out the Windows' and 'Walney Echoes, One, Two, Three'. Many place names around the country are also of Viking origin, such as Whitby and Skegness.

Who was William of Normandy?

William the Conqueror was born in France in 1027, and at the age of seven became Duke of Normandy. When he grew up he claimed that the English king Edward the Confessor, who was a cousin of William's father, had promised him he would inherit the English throne. William's French subjects considered him intelligent and fair, but not surprisingly they also thought he was very ambitious.

William of Normandy at the head of his troops at the Battle of Hastings.

How did the French conquer England?

When Edward the Confessor died in January 1066, William of Normandy did not inherit the English throne. Instead, Harold Godwinson was crowned king. William was furious and sailed with his troops to Pevensey on the south coast of England. Harold's followers had just returned from the north, where they had defeated a Viking invasion, and were too weary to fight properly. They were massacred at the Battle of Hastings, and Harold was killed. England now had French rulers.

Were the English nobles loyal?

Sort of. When Harold was crowned king, they swore an oath of loyalty to him. Then when William the Conqueror was crowned King of England on Christmas Day 1066 at Westminster Abbey – they swore an oath of loyalty to him as well!

How did the Normans rule England?

William the Conqueror brought no ordinary French people to live in England, only an army of 10,000 soldiers led by a handful of nobles. They were expected to rule over a population of 2 million English people – who did not like them very much! So they built castles throughout the land, and ruled from these powerful strongholds.

ONE IN THE EYE FOR HAROLD

The beautiful Bayeux Tapestry records the Norman Conquest in pictures. It shows a soldier plucking an arrow from his eye at the Battle of Hastings, and some historians believe this is Harold. Others claim Harold was killed by four soldiers – one pierced his chest with a lance; a second cut off his head with a sword; a third thrust a javelin into his belly; a fourth cut off his leg. It makes the arrow in the eye sound quite painless!

What was the Domesday Book?

The Domesday Book was a survey carried out by the Normans to record who owned the land and property in England. By the time it was finished in 1086, the great book recorded that over fifty castles had been built throughout the country.

Did life change for the English under Norman rule?

Yes, William removed the English earls and put his own barons in charge of estates dotted around the country. French barons controlled the estates, and rented out the land to English villagers. New laws required workers to live and work on one estate, which they were forbidden to leave.

How were poachers punished?

Punishment for poaching was severe. Stealing deer might be punished by the loss of an eye or a hand. Repeat offending (which was more difficult with only one eye or hand) could be punished by death.

Did people go hunting in Norman times?

In Anglo-Saxon times, poor people relied on hunting for their food, especially in years when the crops failed. But William seized a lot of land and turned it into 'royal forest'. When poor people continued to hunt on the king's land, they were arrested as poachers.

Why did dogs lose their claws?

Some barons ordered the peasants' dogs to have the nails removed from their front paws so that they could not be used for hunting. No wonder there were uprisings in Kent, Wales, the West Country and the north of England.

What sport was played in Norman times?

Some people were fond of an early form of cricket, which they played with wooden or leather balls. The bats were curved sticks called 'crics', an Anglo-Saxon word for a shepherd's crook. Players stood in front of a wicket-gate while others hurled the ball to hit a cross-piece called a 'bail'.

In East Anglia, a noble by the name of Hereward the Wake made a stand against the Norman invaders. When William's men attacked, Hereward managed to escape.

What were the Crusades?

Since the seventh century, many Arabs had followed the teaching of the Muslim prophet Muhammad. Jerusalem was a city holy to both Muslims and Christians, and when it came under Muslim control it became impossible for Christian pilgrims to visit. Jerusalem was defended by the Seljuk Turks, who considered fighting Christians a holy duty. In 1095, Pope Urban II declared war on the Muslims and ordered the Christians to recapture Jerusalem. Many Christian knights headed for the Holy Land to fight what became known as the Crusades. They lasted from 1095 to 1291.

Who had the heart of a lion?

Richard I, who was a descendant of William the Conqueror, ruled England from 1189 to 1199. Although he was born in England, he spoke mostly in French. Many English people called him the 'absent king' because he only ever spent six months of his reign in England. The rest of the time he was away fighting – either in France, or in the Holy Land during the Crusades. His bravery while trying to capture the city of Jerusalem earned him the nickname, Coeur de Lion, or Lionheart.

Who fought in the Crusades?

The Crusades were fought by knights from the aristocratic families of Europe. But the First Crusade was also joined by some 20,000 peasants, led by a fanatical preacher called Peter the Hermit. Most of these peasants were massacred, but the knights were more successful. They captured Jerusalem on July 15, 1099.

Did the crusaders go straight home?

No, the rich knights who fought in the First Crusade set up three new kingdoms in the Holy Land. They ruled over them just like they would a big estate in Europe, collecting taxes from the local people and hiring out land to Arab lords.

HOLY KNIGHTS FIGHT CRUSADES

The Crusades were dominated by two orders of knights – who were also monks! These were the Knights Templar and the Hospitallers Of St John. Both orders had castles, forts and hospitals scattered throughout Europe and the Holy Land. They used them to nurse sick pilgrims, train knights and raise money for the Crusades.

What was the Children's Crusade?

In 1212, thousands of children from France and Germany set off on their own crusade. They believed that if they prayed hard enough, God would help them capture the Holy Land. Clearly, their prayers were insufficient – most were kidnapped by Muslim pirates and sold into slavery, and not a single child made it to Jerusalem.

How did the Turks fight during a battle?

The Turks would rush into battle on horseback, fire a volley of arrows, and retreat immediately. It was a tactic that gradually wore down their opponents. If a knight was well protected by armour, the Turks would often shoot his horse instead.

How did crusaders attack towns?

While laying siege to a town, the crusaders sometimes built huge wooden catapults called mangonels and petrarias. With these, they launched enormous boulders, each of which could kill twenty men at a time.

How did crusaders square-up for a fight?

Crusaders usually fought on horseback, wearing chain mail to protect them from swords and arrows. When surrounded, the knights would dismount and form a large square with their precious horses safely in the centre.

Knights look down on one of the castles built by the Crusaders in the Holy Land.

How did a riding accident unsettle Scotland?

For most of the thirteenth century, the people of Scotland were at peace with the English. Under their own ruler, Alexander III, the Scots enjoyed a golden age. But in 1286 poor Alexander died in a riding accident, leaving Scotland with no heir to the throne. Unable to decide who should be their next king, the Scots asked Edward I, king of England, to choose for them. There were two contenders – John Balliol and Robert the Bruce, Lord of Annandale.

Did Balliol betray Scotland?

Edward I chose John Balliol to be the next king of Scotland, because he secretly hoped that he would help England to invade and conquer the Scots. When Balliol was crowned in 1292, he was made to swear allegiance to England. But Balliol would not betray his new kingdom, and made a secret deal with the French to help him conquer northern England. Edward I lost his patience and in 1296 he decided to invade Scotland.

Who was Toom Tabard?

Marching up to Scotland with his army, Edward I massacred some 20,000 people on the borders. No one was spared, not even women and children. The Scottish army was routed at Dunbar and John Balliol surrendered. He was stripped of his royal insignia and became known as Toom Tabard – which means Empty Jacket.

William Wallace fights at the Battle of Stirling.

Was it wise to insult William Wallace?

Not really. When the young Scot William Wallace was studying with monks in Dundee, the son of the English governor insulted him. Wallace promptly drew his sword and killed him. Five years later, the English sheriff of Lanark murdered Wallace's wife – and he too paid with his life. Wallace then fled to a nearby forest, where he was joined by Scots eager to expel the English from their homeland.

What happened at Stirling?

The forces of Edward I and William Wallace met at Stirling on September 11, 1297. The English outnumbered the Scots three to one, but the Scots knew the countryside around Stirling very well. Wallace's warriors rushed from hiding to surprise the English troops as they were crossing a narrow bridge over the River Forth, and won an amazing victory.

What were the Ragman Rolls?

Every Scottish nobleman was forced to swear allegiance to the king of England. They had to sign a document known as the 'Ragman Rolls'. English people were put into positions of power around Scotland, and it seemed the Scots had lost their independence.

Robert the Bruce watches a spider complete its web.

How was Wallace buried in four places?

Wallace was made the guardian of Scotland, but in 1298 his forces were defeated by the English at the Battle of Falkirk. Wallace was finally captured in 1305 and taken to the Tower of London. He was hung, drawn and quartered – and the four parts of his body were sent to Berwick, Newcastle, Perth and Stirling.

Why won't Scots kill spiders?

In 1306, Robert the Bruce was in exile and the English had seized his castles. According to legend, as he lay down in despair he watched a spider try six times to swing across a gap and finish its web. The Bruce had himself fought six battles without success. When the spider succeeded at the seventh attempt, the Bruce swore to return to Scotland and fight on. Spiders now hold a special place in Scottish hearts!

What happened at Bannockburn?

At Bannockburn, on July 24, 1314, the Bruce lured the English forces of Edward II on to marshy ground, and defeated them once and for all. In 1328, Scotland finally achieved independence from England when the Treaty of Northampton was signed. The Bruce was crowned king but died a year later.

Who was the Bruce?

Robert the Bruce was brought up at the court of Edward I, and his loyalty wavered between the English and his Scottish origins. In 1306, he was crowned king of Scotland by his supporters and war broke out between Scotland and England. By 1314, nearly the whole of Scotland was in his hands.

SCONE STONE GONE

Scottish kings were crowned while sitting on the Stone of Scone, or Stone of Destiny. Nobody knows where this slab of black stone decorated with a cross came from. Some say it was carved in the Middle East, others that it was made by Scottish craftsmen. In 1296, the sacred relic was taken by Edward I. It was not returned to the Scots until 1996. But some people still believe the Scots had tricked Edward I by giving him a false stone!

Richard de Clare, known as Strongbow, became king of Leinster in 1171.

Which king was thrown out for eloping?

Ireland was ruled by a number of 'high kings', and in 1166 they got together to expel Dermot MacMurrough, who was high king of Leinster. He was thrown out for eloping with the daughter of one of the other kings! King Henry II of England saw this as an opportunity to conquer Ireland, and helped MacMurrough to raise an army to attack the high kings and win back his kingdom. MacMurrough was then expected to swear allegiance to the English throne.

What is Castle Hall?

The high kings of Ireland were horrified when Strongbow, a Norman, claimed the throne of Leinster. They refused to give him his inheritance, and Strongbow appealed to Henry II for help. Henry sent his army across the Irish Sea, conquered Ireland and gave Leinster to Strongbow. Then he set up the centre of English rule at Castle Hall in Dublin, and awarded the rest of the land to Norman nobles.

Who was Strongbow?

Strongbow was the nickname of Richard de Clare, a long-legged Norman knight who offered to help MacMurrough win back his throne. He helped him to conquer Dublin in 1170, and to win back the throne of Leinster. Strongbow then married MacMurrough's daughter Aoife. When MacMurrough died in 1171, the long-legged knight inherited his throne and all his wealth and power.

ARMY SPREADS BLACK DEATH

During the 1340s, a terrible army marched across Europe, leaving one in three people dead. It was not an army of soldiers, but an army of rats. The rodents carried a horrific disease called the Black Death. People who were infected started coughing up blood. Red bruises appeared on their skin and lumps as big as tennis balls grew in their armpits. Most died within three days. A lucky few died within hours.

Who improved Irish farming?

After the conquest of Dublin in 1170, many Normans started settling in Ireland. They introduced better farming methods to the Irish countryside, and the country prospered. By 1250, the Irish were exporting food and importing luxury goods like wine and wool.

What did the Normans think of Irish customs?

They liked them so much that they began to adopt them for themselves. They started to speak Irish and took Irish names, and the more Irish they became the more their loyalty to England waned.

Who was Edward the Bruce?

Edward the Bruce was the brother of Robert, and was summoned to Ireland to help the Irish expel the Normans from their land. The people, including some Norman families who now considered themselves to be Irish, welcomed him with open arms.

Why did the Irish starve?

Edward the Bruce was crowned king of Ireland, and led an army of Scots and Irish into battle against the English. In 1318, he was defeated and killed at Dundalk. By now, Ireland was starving as many fields and crops had been burned during the fighting, but English power had been weakened beyond repair.

Who was banned from being Irish?

In 1366, the English king Edward III drew up the Statutes of Kilkenny. Under these laws, English people in Ireland were forbidden to take part in Irish customs or to use the Irish language. Marriages between Irish and English people were also banned.

Who lost their heads?

Edward III gave the English permission to chop off the head of any Irishman they suspected of stealing from them. Despite such behaviour, or perhaps because of it, English influence on Ireland continued to dwindle.

Who was beyond the Pale?

By 1400, England controlled only one twentieth of Ireland. A century later, this had shrunk even further to a narrow strip of land around Dublin. This land was known as the English Pale.

An Irish farmer harvests his crops.

Did the Hundred Years' War last that long?

The Hundred Years' War was a series of battles between the kings and knights of England and France that lasted from 1337 to 1453 – a total of 116 years. In 1328, Charles IV of France died without leaving an heir. King Edward III of England claimed he should have the French throne. He was descended from an earlier French king and he already ruled Gascony in France. But Philip the Strong was given the French crown, and in 1337 he also seized Gascony. Edward and his knights sailed for France and the Hundred Years' War began.

Which farmers went to war?

The English army included many Welsh and English farmers. During peacetime, they were paid to do military training, and were punished if they did not train enough. During wartime, their pay increased dramatically and they received rations for food and clothing.

What kind of weapons made the English famous?

During the Hundred Years' War, English archers became famous for their deadly use of the longbow. Originally used for hunting in Wales, the longbow took years of practice to master.

How many horses did a knight have?

The richer a knight was, the more horses he had. But every knight, even the poorest one, needed to have at least two. One, called a palfrey, was used for riding around the countryside and hunting. The other, known as a destrier, was the precious war-horse reserved for battle.

Which horses were the best?

The horses of Normandy were believed to be the best in the world. A knight's horse was considered his most precious possession, and the knights of France and England favoured the horses of Normandy above all others.

Henry V at the Battle of Agincourt in 1415.

Edward, the Black Prince, fighting in his famous black armour.

Who was known as the Black Prince?

The most famous knight of the Hundred Years' War was Prince Edward, son of Edward III. He led the English to victory at the Battle of Crécy in 1346 – when he was only sixteen! Edward became known as the Black Prince because he fought in a magnificent suit of black armour.

How did the Hundred Years' War end?

In 1422, both Henry V and Charles VI died. Henry's son was too young to rule, and when they realized that the English had no able leader the French took full advantage. They resumed hostilities and by 1453 had expelled the English from France once and for all.

Whose wedding brought England and France together?

Henry V became king of England in 1413, and two years later defeated the forces of the French king Charles VI at the famous Battle of Agincourt. Because Henry was partly French, Charles later declared him heir to the French throne. Henry married Charles's daughter, and the French and English royal families were united.

Did people live long in Medieval times?

In a time when war was constantly being fought, disease was rife, and medicine was basic to say the least. People were considered old when they got to their forties. Fifty was thought very old. If you lived to be seventy, you were thought to be … lucky!

WOMAN BURNT AS WITCH

A French peasant called Joan of Arc believed God had called her to save France from the English. She led an army to the city of Orleans, which the English had been attacking for five months. Dressed in a suit of armour, she commanded an amazing French victory. Joan was later captured and burnt at the stake as a witch. Centuries after her death, she was made a saint.

Joan of Arc.

What was the Spanish Armada?

The Armada was a group of some 130 warships that King Philip II of Spain sent as an invasion force to conquer England in 1588. The term 'armada' means 'fleet of armed ships'. The Spanish were so proud of their fleet that they called it the 'Grande Armada', meaning the big fleet. Some of them were even prouder, and called it the 'Invincible Armada'. Unfortunately for them, it wasn't!

King Philip II of Spain.

Why did Philip II want to conquer England?

Since Elizabeth I became queen in 1558, England had followed the Protestant religion. Under Philip II, Spain was a Catholic nation. Philip considered it his holy duty to free England from its Protestant rulers and restore it to the arms of the Roman Catholic Church. He was also fed up with English ships attacking Spanish vessels and robbing them of their loot!

What did Elizabeth do to Catholics?

Elizabeth made life very difficult for English Catholics, particularly in times of war. They were fined if they refused to attend services in Protestant churches. Those that secretly attended mass in Catholic churches ran the risk of imprisonment and possibly death.

English ships attack the Spanish Armada.

What was Philip II like?

Philip II came to the throne of Spain in 1556, at the age of twenty-eight. He was a devout man, who spent a lot of time praying and fasting in his magnificent palace outside Madrid called El Escorial.

Who had bad indigestion?

As a prince, Philip II married Queen Mary of England in a bid to strengthen links between Spain and England. After Mary died in 1558, Philip became an increasingly bitter man. In later life he suffered a disease brought on by eating too many rich foods, and had terrible trouble sleeping.

What did the Armada carry?

As well as cannons and arms, the Armada's ships had to carry enormous quantities of food and water. Some ships carried horses and mules, and had large tents on board to shelter the many soldiers who would lead the invasion of England.

What were zebras?

Small vessels called zebras were used to carry messages around the Armada, from one ship to another. They also acted as spying ships, galloping ahead of the main fleet to scout for enemy vessels.

Who singed the king's beard?

In 1587, the ships of the Armada were anchored in the Spanish port of Cadiz. Sir Francis Drake, one of Elizabeth's finest captains, set some old ships on fire and steered them into the port – where they set light to many Spanish ships. Drake laughingly called this 'singeing the King of Spain's beard'.

Did the Armada conquer England?

No. Of the 130 ships that set sail from Lisbon, only 60 ever returned to Spanish ports. Some had been sunk by the English fleet as they struggled through the English Channel. Others were wrecked by storms on the rocky shores of Ireland and Scotland as they tried to escape. Some 20,000 men lost their lives in the attempt to conquer England.

How did the Spanish leaders take the news?

The ragged remnants of the Armada arrived home with the sailors and soldiers dying of starvation and horrible diseases. The fleet's commander Medina Sedonia returned safely but died soon after, a broken man. It is said, on the other hand, that King Philip II received the news of his loss with the calm of a true king.

Queen Elizabeth I of England.

NUMBER ONE ENEMY KNIGHTED

Francis Drake received permission from Elizabeth I to plunder Spanish ships returning to Europe from the Americas. His pirate raids brought the queen enormous quantities of gold, silver, spices and other treasures. This made him the number one enemy of Spain, and when Elizabeth knighted Drake, the Spanish ambassador was red with rage.

Who were the Pilgrim Fathers?

What ship did the pilgrims sail on?

The pilgrims travelled on a small ship called the *Mayflower*. Only twenty-seven metres long, it was a craft built to travel close to the coast of Europe, not to cross an ocean. Its passengers suffered terribly during the journey, as they were jammed together in close quarters and hurled about by rough seas.

Who had a brief glimpse of America?

One of the pilgrims, a woman called Dorothy Bradford, fell overboard and drowned just after she first gazed at the coast of America.

On August 5, 1620, a group of 102 men and women sailed from Southampton, England, in search of a new and better life in America. Their arrival and settlement in what is now New England was part of a movement across the Atlantic that had begun in 1607. Thirty-five of the group followed a religion called the English Separatist Church. They went to America to escape religious persecution. As a result, the whole group that left England in 1620 came to be known as the Pilgrim Fathers.

Pilgrims make their way ashore at Plymouth Bay in what is now Massachusetts, USA.

Why were the pilgrims off course?

The captain of the ship was aiming to land in Virginia, which already had English settlements. But strong winds blew the *Mayflower* off course and it was forced to anchor at a bay in Cape Cod, Massachusetts. The pilgrims named it Plymouth Bay, after Plymouth Sound in England where their voyage had begun.

How did the pilgrims survive?

The Pilgrim Fathers reached America in December 1620, a harsh time of year to start a colony. They built huts to shelter from the freezing weather, then searched desperately for food. Luckily, local Native Americans came to their aid and taught them the skills they needed to survive.

Who was John Smith?

An adventurer, sailor and soldier of fortune, Captain John Smith became the leader of the Virginia settlement. He was captured by Algonquians, and taken to a place called Werowocomoco. The Algonquians held a great feast in his honour, but then a group of warriors grabbed Smith. He was saved only when a chief's daughter named Pocahontas begged for his life.

How did the Native Americans help?

The Native Americans showed the settlers how to hunt and trap. They taught them how to make maple sugar, how to sew warm moccasins for their feet, and how to build canoes.

Who celebrated Thanksgiving?

In 1621, the Pilgrims harvested their first crops. To celebrate, they caught and cooked birds then found only in America – turkeys! The feast would become an annual celebration called Thanksgiving, which is still a very important date in the American calendar.

Were the pilgrims the first English settlers in America?

No. In April 1607, three ships had reached the east coast of America, and anchored at Chesapeake Bay, Virginia. The colonists on board had built a settlement which they called Jamestown after King James I, ruler of England and Scotland.

Who were the Algonquians?

Some of the Native Americans that helped the English settlers survive belonged to the Algonquian nation. They lived around the rivers of Virginia, hunting and growing crops. They happily traded with the settlers, exchanging food and furs for tools.

What was the Jacobite Rebellion?

In 1707, England and Scotland joined together under the Act of Union to form Great Britain. The first king of the new union was George I, who was a Protestant and a member of the Hanover family. The Hanovers were German, and George barely spoke English. Many Catholics, especially those in Scotland, believed members of the Stuart family had a stronger claim to the throne. Matters came to a head in an uprising called the Jacobite Rebellion.

Who was the Old Pretender?

James Edward Stuart was known as the Old Pretender because he 'pretended to', or claimed, the English throne. The word Jacobite comes from the Latin for James. The Old Pretender was helped to lead a rebellion against George I by the French king, Louis XIV, who was also a Catholic. But the Jacobite Rebellion of 1715 was crushed.

Who was the Young Pretender?

Bonnie Prince Charlie, the son of James Edward Stuart, was known as the Young Pretender. He was born and educated in Rome, but the Jacobites hoped that he would come to claim the British throne. In July 1745, he landed in Scotland with only seven followers and said: 'I am come home'.

What did the Scots think of Charlie?

Bonnie Prince Charlie was a hero to the Scottish people even when he was still living abroad. They had written songs and poems about him, and placed their hopes in him. When he landed in Scotland, people rushed from the Highlands to fight with him for the British throne.

What weapons did the highlanders use?

Highland warriors used long, two-handed swords called claymores. They also had short daggers called dirks. During a battle they would protect themselves with small shields called torges.

Scottish Highlanders in battle against the Duke of Cumberland's troops at Culloden.

What happened at Culloden?

Culloden was one of the bloodiest battles fought on British soil. On April 16, 1746, an English army led by George II's son, the Duke of Cumberland, met Bonnie Prince Charlie's followers on Culloden Moor. Charlie's Highlanders were freezing and exhausted from their long march, and over 1,000 of them were massacred.

Who was the Butcher?

The Duke of Cumberland became known as the Butcher. To make sure the Jacobites never tried to invade England again, he decided to wipe out the Highlanders. All the men left on the battlefield of Culloden were slaughtered.

Who had their bagpipes banned?

After Culloden, Highlanders were forbidden to use tartan, wear kilts, or carry guns. They were not even allowed to play their bagpipes. Most were evicted from their houses and many emigrated to Canada in search of a better life. That is why there are so many Canadians of Scottish descent.

PRINCE DRESSES AS MAID

Bonnie Prince Charlie escaped from the slaughter at Culloden, but £30,000 was offered for his capture. Despite the size of the reward, nobody betrayed him. The Young Pretender finally escaped by disguising himself as the maid of a Scot named Flora Macdonald, and pretending to have the name Betty Burke!

Bonnie Prince Charlie.

Who was a long way from home?

By September 1745, Bonnie Prince Charlie had gathered enough followers to march on England. They defeated the English at Prestonpans, and scored another victory at Falkirk. But as the Jacobites reached Derby in England, they started to falter. Far from home, they missed the support of their people.

What was the British Raj?

A Britsh Army soldier in India.

The word *raj* is Indian for reign or rule. As British traders made more money, so Britain began to conquer parts of India. Some territories were conquered by force, like the Raj of Berar which was home to five million people and countless treasures. A few kingdoms remained independent, but they were ruled by Indian princes who were protected by the British. In 1783 the East India Company started running the administration of India on behalf of the British government. This began a period of rule known as the British Raj.

What was the East India Company?

As far back as 1693, a British company called the East India Company was controlling trade between India and the rest of the British Empire. It made large amounts of money by trading in goods like gold, silk and precious stones. It also made the British government lots of money by collecting taxes. By 1767, the East India Company was paying the government £400,000 a year. The company was the main driving force behind the British conquest of lands in Asia.

How did life change in India?

The British saw themselves as the rulers of India. English replaced Persian as the language of government. In 1853, the first Indian railway was built. But such things had little impact on most of India's 200 million inhabitants, who continued to live traditional village lives.

What did missionaries do?

Christian missionaries were allowed to teach and preach to the Indians. But the Indian population already had strong religious beliefs. Most people were Hindus, and most of the others were Muslims.

What upset the Indian people?

The removal of many local princes caused great alarm. The British also took away a lot of land, and introduced heavy taxes. But worst of all, Indian soldiers suspected that the British were trying to convert them to Christianity.

Was the British Army all British?

By 1857, 40,000 British soldiers were stationed in the Indian region. But the army also contained 200,000 Asians. They had joined up because they received regular pay and enjoyed better working conditions than most Indians.

An Indian soldier in the British Army.

How did cows and pigs start a rebellion?

In 1857, Indian soldiers known as sepoys were given new rifles to use. To load them, soldiers had to bite the ends off cartridges which they believed were sealed with cow and pig fat. This horrified all the sepoys. The Hindus believed cows were sacred and the Muslims believed pigs were unclean. When British officers ignored their complaints, the sepoys mutinied.

What cities were captured in the Sepoy Mutiny?

The sepoys took Meerut and Cawnpore, and captured Delhi and Lucknow after long sieges. They proclaimed a local ruler called Bahadur Shah the emperor of all India. It looked as if Britain would lose the jewel of its empire. But the outnumbered British rallied and somehow restored their rule.

Did things get better for the Indians?

The Sepoy Mutiny came as a big shock to the British, who had been hopelessly ignorant of Indian discontent. British people were forbidden to seize any more Indian land after the mutiny. New laws were also passed giving Indians the right to practise their religions and customs.

Who became civil servants?

In 1858, the East India Company was abolished and a special ministry was set up in London to look after India. Many Indians were now given jobs in the civil service.

GREAT SOUL BRINGS INDEPENDENCE

The Indians did not gain independence from Britain until 1947, following the efforts of a leader named Mahatma (which means 'great soul') Gandhi. He hated violence and taught his followers to protest peacefully. Gandhi went on hunger strikes and was frequently arrested, but was rewarded when India gained independence.

What was the 'Scramble for Africa'?

By the latter half of the nineteenth century, many European countries had become industrialized. They looked to Africa as a source of raw materials and a market for their goods. This started the 'Scramble for Africa' – a time when European nations conquered different parts of Africa and turned them into colonies. By the late 1800s, nearly the whole of Africa had been carved up between the European powers.

Which parts of Africa did Britain colonize?

Between 1882 and 1902, Britain laid claim to countries including Egypt, Rhodesia (now Zimbabwe), Nyasaland (now Malawi), Uganda, Kenya, Ashanti (now Ghana) and Nigeria. The colonies provided England with raw materials such as rubber and timber. Gold could also be obtained from West Africa, while the mines of South Africa were rich in diamonds.

Who invaded Zululand?

In 1879, a British army under the command of Lieutenant General Frederick Augustus Thesiger, Earl of Chelmsford, invaded Zululand, a country in south-east Africa. But they met ferocious resistance from the armies of a people called Zulus.

Boers – Dutch settlers – in southern Africa. They fought against the invading British to protect the lands they had settled.

Who won the Battle of Khambula?

Who was outnumbered at Khambula?

On March 29, 1789 several hundred British soldiers led by Colonel H. E. Wood were attacked by 25,000 Zulus at a place called Khambula. The Zulus employed their famous 'horns of the beast' movement, advancing on Wood's men who were stationed in a carefully chosen spot on top of a hill.

What were the horns of the beast?

Zulu warriors used a traditional method of attack called the 'horns of the beast'. Two regiments, representing the beasts' horns, moved in a pincer movement around the side of the enemy. More regiments, representing the belly of the beast, then moved in to crush anyone in their way.

What did the Zulus chant at the British?

As they neared the British troops, the Zulus taunted them. They called out 'Don't run away, Johnny, we want to talk to you. We're the boys from Ishandlwana.'

What did the Zulus do at Ishandlwana?

The Zulus surprised the British at a mountain named Ishandlwana on January 21, 1879. Under the guidance of their leader Cetshwayo, the Zulus destroyed a British regiment.

The British were well prepared, and well armed with cannons and rifles. As the Zulus started to close their pincer movement, the British unleashed a hail of bullets. Over 3,000 Zulus lost their lives that night while the British lost only thirty-two soldiers.

British soldiers firing a Maxim gun.

What happened to the Zulus?

The terrible defeat at Khambula turned the tide of war against Cetshwayo and his brave warriors. They kept on fighting the British, but their pride had been broken and they fought out of despair for their homeland. In 1906, the last Zulu revolt was crushed.

ZAMBEZI TREASURE UP FOR GRABS

In 1888, an African king called Lobengula escaped from advancing British troops with a hoard of treasure including gold, diamonds and ivory. The king hid his loot somewhere on the banks of the Zambezi River, but died before he could return to claim it. Some say it is still hidden there, waiting for someone to find it.

Knights
and Castles

What was a motte-and-bailey?

Many of the first Norman castles had a wooden building, called a keep, built on a high mound called a 'motte'. This was protected by a ditch and a wall of earth, which also surrounded a courtyard known as the 'bailey'. This was called a motte-and-bailey castle.

How did William conquer England?

By building strong castles, William was able to conquer a nation of 2 million people with a force of only 10,000 men. The English at this time had few castles from which they could defend their land.

Which tapestry shows a castle?

The Bayeux Tapestry, started in 1067, shows William's men building a castle at Hastings. Two of the builders appear to be settling an argument – by fighting with their shovels!

Who carried a portable castle?

When the Normans, led by William the Conqueror, invaded England in 1066, they brought with them the wooden parts of a portable castle. They landed at Pevensey, in East Sussex, and had put their castle together by the following day.

What did you do if the king wanted to build a castle on your land?

You moved! When William the Conqueror had Lincoln Castle built in 1068, a total of 166 houses were pulled down to make room for it.

DEVILS AND WICKED MEN

A writer living at the time of the Normans noted: 'They filled the whole land with these castles. They sorely burdened the unhappy people of the country with forced labour on the castles. And when the castles were made, they filled them with devils and wicked men.'

Which bishop designed the Tower of London?

A Norman Knight

The White Tower, the oldest part of the Tower of London, was built for William in 1078. It was designed by Gundulf, the Bishop of Rochester. He had earned a reputation for designing castles by building one beside his cathedral.

What did you do if the king visited your castle?

You welcomed him warmly! William had made it law that he could occupy the castle of any of his barons whenever he wished.

A LOOK AT THE BOOK

William wished to know exactly what he had conquered. So in 1086 his surveyors produced the Domesday Book, which recorded the sources of rent and taxes in his kingdom. It listed estates, livestock and 50 different castles.

How important were castles?

A writer of the twelfth century described Britain's royal castles as the 'bones of the kingdom'.

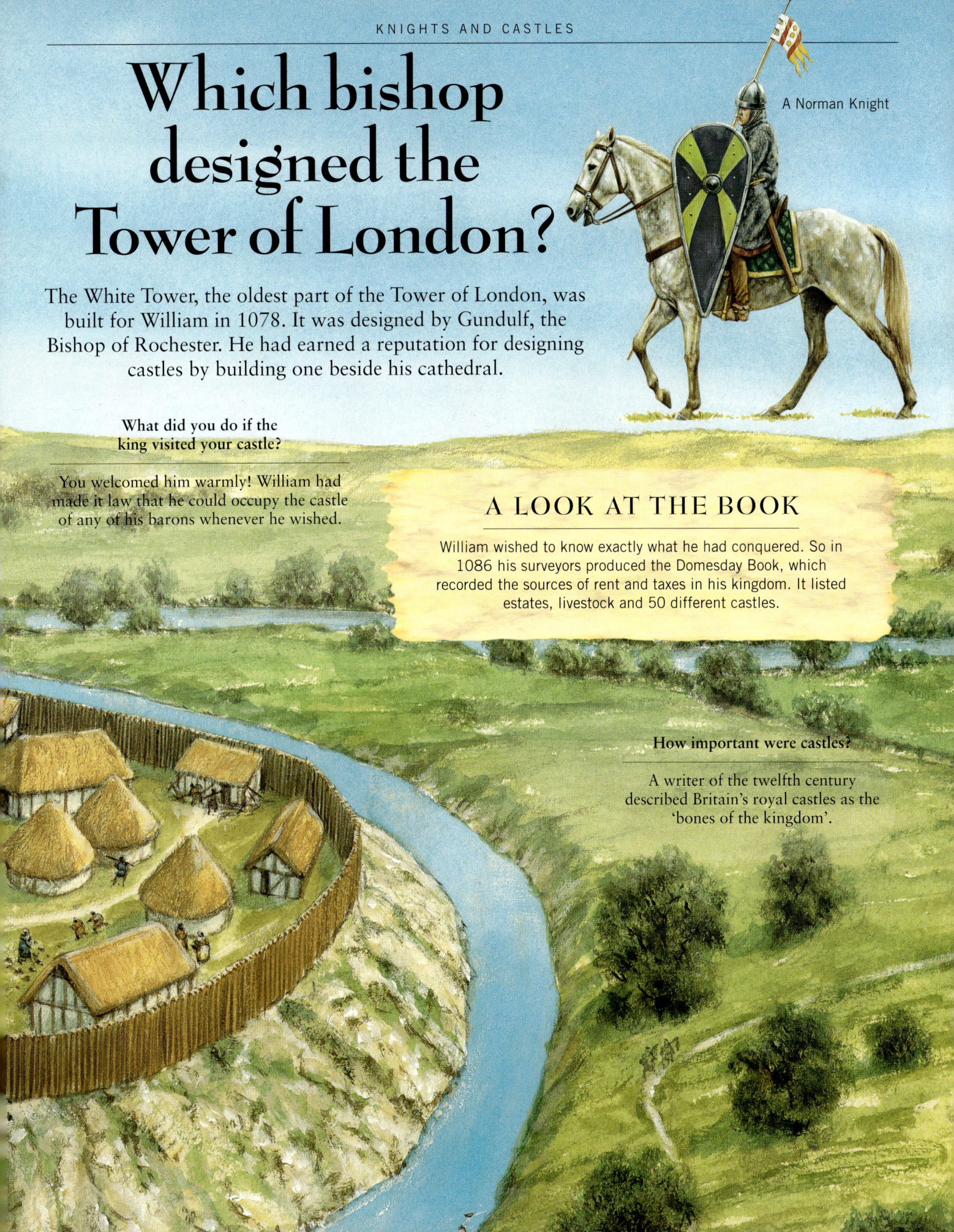

How many men did it take to build a castle?

In 1296 Caernarvon Castle was under construction by Europe's finest castle architect, Master James of St George. His workers included 400 stonemasons, 1,000 labourers, 200 carters and 30 carpenters and metalworkers. In the summer of the previous year there were also some 3,500 builders working on Beaumaris Castle.

Which king's builders went on strike?

In 1303 carpenters and ditchers refused to work for King Edward I at Dunfermline Castle because he owed them so much money for work on his other castles.

How long did it take to build a castle?

Wooden motte-and bailey castles could be built in under a fortnight, but stone castles were a different matter. One of Edward's Welsh castles, Harlech, took over seven years to complete and builders worked on Beaumaris Castle for 35 years without finishing it.

What machines did builders use?

The only machines medieval builders had to help them construct their amazing castles were simple cranes, pulleys and wheelbarrows.

Medieval builders use a crane and an early form of scaffolding to put the finishing touches to this castle.

Were castle walls always grey?

Lime was sometimes used to paint castle walls white so that their dazzling towers could be seen from miles away. This was how the White Tower at the Tower of London got its name. Henry III ordered longer gutters for the Tower, to stop rainwater marking its white walls.

A medieval stone castle

Why did castle staircases spiral clockwise?

A clockwise spiral staircase allowed a defender to retreat backwards up the stairs while swinging his sword with his right hand at a pursuer below. It was almost impossible for the man chasing him to swing a blow – unless he was left-handed!

How thick were castle walls?

Stone castles were built with walls over three metres thick. These could withstand missiles fired from enormous catapults. At Dover Castle, in Kent, some walls were over six metres thick.

What did gargoyles spit out at Beaumaris Castle?

At Beaumaris, sewage from the garderobes travelled down shafts then out through the mouths of carved gargoyles and into the moat. In 1306 there were complaints that the gargoyles' mouths had become blocked.

Why did the castle moat stink?

The 'garderobes', or castle toilets, were small, stone rooms with a hole in the floor. They were often positioned over a shaft that led directly into the moat.

DRESS TO IMPRESS

Kings could force labourers to work on their castles. During Edward III's building work at Windsor Castle, stonemasons had to travel down from Yorkshire. They were made to dress in bright red clothes – so that they could not sneak away.

Bees buzzing around their bee-hive.

Where were bees kept?

Bees were kept in straw hives on the castle walls. Their honey was used to sweeten food and drink.

Which king had double-glazing?

As the medieval period went on, more and more castles installed glass in their windows. Henry III even had double-glazing at Windsor Castle.

A royal party arrives at a castle, announced by a herald.

BUTTER BY DESIGN

In medieval times English kings also ruled lands in France. Richard the Lionheart built a magnificent castle called Château Gaillard in Normandy. He was so pleased with its design that he boasted he could defend the castle even if its walls were made of butter.

Were castles fit for kings and queens?

At Windsor Castle, Edward III had six private chambers, one large enough to contain 20 windows and another painted in azure, gold, green and vermillion. The queen had four chambers, including a dancing room and a chamber covered with mirrors.

How did they tell the time at Windsor Castle?

Windsor Castle contained the first mechanical clock known in England.

How did people grow grapes?

In the 1100s Gerald of Wales describes his estate at Manorbier Castle as including a deep fish-pond, a beautiful orchard and a vineyard. The climate in medieval times was slightly hotter than today, and conditions were ideal for growing grapes to make wine.

Who lived in castles?

Castles were normally the homes of kings and barons, rather than knights. But royalty only visited a castle occasionally, before moving on to the next of their many homes. During their visits the castle became home to crowds of workers, cooks and servants.

Were pets kept in castles?

Yes, lords and ladies kept pets including dogs, cats, squirrels, mice, songbirds and even monkeys, bears and leopards. They also had horses, hounds and hawks for hunting, which was the favourite pastime of most lords.

A medieval king watches while his queen feeds her pet monkey.

Where did a king keep his elephant?

As well as being a castle fortress, the Tower of London was an important prison and a zoo for exotic animals! In one of the towers, called the Lion Tower, Henry III kept an elephant.

How did a king communicate with his servants?

Henry III had a speaking tube known as the 'king's ear' through which he could talk to his servants. It linked the king's solar, or private chamber, with the great hall at Winchester Castle.

Who lived around the castle?

Many peasants lived around the castle walls, because it was a place of security in dangerous times. The castle estate also provided land for farmers. Many of them were 'serfs', who were owned and controlled by the lord on whose land they worked. The serfs farmed the lord's land and raised livestock. They divided their produce between the lord and themselves.

What services did serfs perform for the castle?

Serfs living around the castle were given different duties to help with building, maintaining and defending the castle. At one castle a villager had to fetch basins of water so that the knights could wash. In return, he received bread, wine and the first choice of kitchen scraps.

How were taxes paid?

The peasants who lived on the lord's land had to visit the castle to pay their taxes. These included the 'wood-penny' tax which people paid for the right to collect firewood from the estate's forests.

Who travelled with trunks?

Serfs living on the estate of Bamburgh Castle, Northumberland, were expected to bring a tree trunk to the castle once a year to help with building works. This tax was known as 'trunkage'.

Serfs work in the fields around the castle.

GOING, GOING, GONG

In a medieval castle the toilet was known as the 'gong'. The 'gong farmer' was the servant who emptied the pits at the bottom of the latrines, using a bucket and shovel. In 1326 a gong farmer named Richard the Raker died after falling into one of these pits!

Who needed plenty of trousers?

A servant called the ale conner tested the castle's beer by pouring it onto a wooden bench then sitting in it. If he soon found himself glued to the bench, he declared that the ale was bad. If he could stand up, he declared the ale to be good.

A castle mill.

Did castle servants live in squalor?

Not necessarily. At Sir John Fastolf's castle at Caister, in Norfolk, the cook, gardener and porter each had separate bedrooms – equipped with feather beds, sheets and curtains.

How did a windmill turn a profit?

Many castles, such as Edward I's castle at Dover, had their own windmills. Peasants had to grind their corn at the lord's windmill, and, in return, the lord kept some of the flour. They also had to pay to bake bread in the castle oven!

Who was allowed to fish?

The lord of the manor only allowed certain people to fish in the ponds on the castle estate. One lord only gave fishing rights to pregnant women!

How did Edward I keep himself amused?

Edward I travelled to his daughter's wedding in 1296 with entertainers including his personal jester called Tom the Fool, a fiddler, a female acrobat, three actors and a bagpipe player.

The king's jester.

Did jesters wear shoes with curly toes?

A jester at the court of William Rufus was known as 'Horner' because he stuffed the long toes of his shoes and curled them up like a ram's horn.

Were kings really entertained by jesters?

Yes, many kings kept dwarves, fools and jesters to make them laugh at feasts and celebrations. One jester was granted an estate in Suffolk on condition that he entertained Henry II each Christmas with 'a leap, a whistle and a fart'.

How big were the ovens in the castle kitchen?

King John ordered new kitchens to be built at his castles, with ovens big enough to roast two or three oxen.

Which groom died from indigestion?

At the wedding feast of Prince Lionel in 1368, 30 courses were served. The food included suckling pig with crab, heron with carp, eel pies, peacocks with cabbage, pickled ox-tongue and meats covered with gold leaf. The bloated groom died four months later.

Who looked after the jesters?

After 1502, there was an official in the royal household called the Keeper of the King's Fools.

Why were there sharks' teeth on salt-cellars?

Kings and lords lived in fear of being poisoned, and employed tasters to test their food. Sharks' teeth, known as 'serpents' tongues', were believed to sweat when placed near poisonous food.

Did people have table manners?

One book advised diners: 'It is improper to scratch your head on the table; to remove from your neck fleas and other vermin and kill them in front of others; and to scratch or pull at scabs.' Another advised against stroking cats and dogs beneath the table.

Were there really 'four and twenty blackbirds baked in a pie'?

Yes there were. As a novelty, castle chefs sometimes baked an empty pie then lifted off the crust and filled it with live birds before serving. Roast swans and peacocks were also put back into their skins for presentation.

WINE INTO WATER

A deep well was vital in a castle to supply drinking water during a siege. When Exeter Castle was besieged in 1136 and their water ran out, the occupants of the castle used wine to drink, bake bread and put out fires.

Were castle meals fit for a king?

They certainly could be! Preparing to spend the Christmas of 1206 at Winchester Castle, King John ordered the local sheriff to provide 1,500 chickens, 5,000 eggs, 20 oxen, 100 pigs and 100 sheep. Henry III made more exotic demands for a banquet at Gloucester, which included 10,000 eels, 36 swans, 34 peacocks and 90 boars.

Lord, ladies, bishops and barons enjoy a feast fit for a king.

Which bishop escaped from the Tower of London?

The Bishop of Durham, Ranulf Flambard, became the first prisoner to escape from the Tower of London, where he was imprisoned in 1106. He sent out for some food and drink, then offered wine to his gaolers until they fell asleep. Ranulf then used a rope, which had been concealed in a wine barrel, to lower himself through a window to the ground. His servants were waiting with a boat on the Thames, and the bishop escaped to France.

What instruments of torture were used in castle dungeons?

Racks stretched victims until their limbs popped from their sockets; thumbscrews and iron boots crushed thumbs and feet; hot irons branded the flesh; pincers tore nails from fingers; bridles held a prisoner's tongue; and a press crushed a prisoner's whole body, with more weights added each day until he or she confessed.

What was an oubliette?

Oubliette comes from the French word meaning 'forgotten'. The oubliette was a tiny cell at the back of the castle dungeon where unwanted prisoners were thrown and forgotten.

How were rich prisoners treated?

They were often treated as guests and kept in great comfort in the castle until a ransom was paid for them. Some prisoners even signed an agreement, promising to behave chivalrously at the castle until their ransom was received.

How did people stand trial?

In the early Middle Ages, some people accused of a crime faced 'trial by ordeal'. They had to grip a bar of red-hot iron. Their burns were then bandaged for three days. When they were unwrapped, any sign of infection proved that they were guilty.

Why should a serf return a hawk?

Hawking was a favourite pastime of the rich. Any serf who found a hawk and failed to return it to its wealthy owner was punished by having the bird peck six ounces of flesh from his breast.

A prisoner in his dungeon hugs himself to try and keep warm.

How was someone hung, drawn and quartered?

Traitors were first 'hung', then cut down before they died. Next they were 'drawn', having their intestines cut out and held up in front of them. When they finally died, their bodies were 'quartered' – cut into four pieces.

A thief sits in the stocks, covered with the rotting fruit and vegetables that passers-by have thrown at him.

Who had their ears nailed?

Thieves were locked into wooden frames, called stocks or pillories, where people could pelt them with rotten fruit. Sometimes, their ears were nailed to the wood.

Whose screams were heard from Berkeley Castle?

On the night of September 21, 1327, the disgraced King Edward II was murdered in the dungeon at Berkeley Castle in Gloucestershire. His screams could be heard from the village beyond the castle walls.

THE YOUNG PRINCES

The skeletons of two young boys were found buried in the Tower of London in 1674. They were thought to be the sons of Edward IV, 12-year-old Edward and 10-year-old Richard. The young princes had disappeared in 1483, enabling Richard III to take the throne.

What was 'Greek Fire'?

When attacking a castle, some armies used an explosive material known as 'Greek Fire'. It was placed in jars and barrels and fired from catapults to explode among the castle inhabitants. Greek Fire contained sulphur, tartar, pitch, salt and oil. One observer noted that it smelt foul and could only be put out with vinegar. It was also sometimes fired from hand pumps – the first flamethrowers!

This enormous catapult could hurl huge boulders over or into castle walls.

Who ordered some pigs?

When besieging Rochester Castle in 1215, King John sent an order for 'forty bacon pigs of the fattest and least good for eating, to bring fire beneath the tower'.

How were messages returned?

At the siege of Auberoche in 1345, a messenger was caught sneaking messages out from the besieged castle. His messages were hung around his neck, and he was placed in the sling of a catapult and fired back over the castle walls.

Did you need much equipment to besiege a castle?

A book published in England in 1489 said that you needed the following equipment to lay siege to a castle: 248 guns; 13,500 kg of gunpowder; 2,200 stones; 200,000 crossbow quarrels; 1,000 shovels and 200 lanterns.

Who set light to cats, mice and birds?

One medieval expert on sieges suggested tying burning ropes to cats and mice, and sending these 'incendiary animals' into a besieged castle through the drains. In the 1260s Simon de Montfort planned to set light to London by tying flaming torches to the talons of birds.

What use is a dead horse?

In 1339 French attackers besieging Edward III's castle at Flanders launched dead horses and cattle over the walls. A painting from this time shows a horse being fired from a catapult.

When did it rain manure?

At a siege in 1422 the attackers used a catapult to fire 2,000 cartloads of manure over the castle walls.

THE LION KING

At the siege of Roxburgh in 1460, James II of Scotland was killed by a Lion! One of his own bombards – which was known as The Lion – exploded, and a piece of the barrel cut his thigh-bone in two.

How did a mine work?

Miners from an attacking army dug a mine, or tunnel, beneath the walls of a besieged castle, propping up the walls of the mine with wooden supports. The miners then filled the tunnel with brushwood and grease and set light to it. The props burnt, the tunnel collapsed and the castle wall above it fell into the hole.

Soldiers set light to the touch-hole of a bombard.

What is Muckle Meg?

Bombards were enormous cannons used to fire missiles at castle walls, making a noise that could be heard over 6.5 km away. One famous example can still be seen at Edinburgh Castle. It weighs 6,000 kg and is called Mons Meg, or 'the great iron murderer Muckle Meg'.

DON'T BE SQUARE

Early castles had square towers, which were easily damaged by catapults and had a narrow range of vision. Later castles were built with round towers. These deflected missiles and gave the defenders a much better view of their attackers.

A moated castle with specially designed round towers.

How did straw kill a knight in armour?

In 1417 Sir Edward Springhouse tried to scale the walls of the castle at Caen, in France, but the defenders pushed his ladder away. He fell to the ground and lay as helpless in his heavy armour as an upturned tortoise. So the French dropped burning straw on him and roasted him alive!

How useful were moats?

The castle moat was an excellent defence, as it had to be filled in before attackers could reach the castle walls. The moat also prevented miners tunnelling beneath the castle walls, because it flooded their tunnels.

Who tried to barge into a castle?

Kenilworth Castle was so well defended by the waters of a lake and moat that when Henry III's son Prince Edward attacked it in 1266, he had to use barges to reach the walls.

Castle inhabitants attempt to foil the battering-ram by softening its blow with an enormous 'cushion'.

How do you stop a battering-ram battering?

Sometimes the castle inhabitants lowered down enormous 'cushions' filled with feathers, rope and wool, to soften the blows of the battering-ram. They also used an enormous forked stick to stop the ram from swinging.

Did castle defenders use siege engines?

Yes, at the siege of Kenilworth Castle both attackers and defenders fired so many rocks that many of them collided and shattered in mid-air.

Why did the garrison put down dishes of water?

If attackers tried to tunnel under the castle walls, then the vibrations they caused would create ripples in the dishes of water, alerting the soldiers in the besieged castle.

Why were dove-cotes built into castle walls?

Doves were used to send messages, which was often the only way to send for help when a castle was surrounded and under siege.

What was a murder-hole?

A murder-hole was a gap in the ceiling of a passageway, particularly in the castle gate-house. The defenders in rooms above the passage could drop missiles down through the murder-hole on to attackers who had entered below.

Who used chemical warfare?

Some castle defenders used chemical warfare by throwing gas bombs made from sulphur, pitch and horses' hooves! These landed among attackers and released their choking fumes.

A soldier pours boiling water through a murder-hole on to an enemy.

How did squires get big muscles?

They practised fighting using weapons which had extra weights added, so that the exercise made them stronger.

What were pages and squires?

When they were seven years old, the sons of knights and nobles were often sent to the household of a lord to serve as a 'page'. The page waited at table, and learned how to behave properly at the castle. At the age of 14, the page might become a 'squire', the personal servant of a knight. He assisted him at war and in tournaments, and learned how to fight, joust, hunt, sing and dance – so that one day he too could become a knight.

What was a quintain?

The quintain was a revolving dummy with a shield on one side and a sword or sandbag on the other. A squire practised jousting by striking the dummy's shield, but had to ride past quickly enough or the sandbag would swing around and knock him off his horse.

How were pages expected to behave?

One book advised pages: 'Do not sigh, or belch, or with puffing and blowing cast foul breath upon your lord.'

Did pages do any cleaning?

Yes, they did many household chores. But they were advised: 'Do not lick a dish with your tongue to get at the dust.'

Squires fight one another piggyback, to build strength and weaponry skills.

What was a knight?

A knight was an armoured warrior who fought on horseback. Knights swore an oath of loyalty to a lord. They promised to fight for him and, in exchange, they received land, money and protection from the lord.

At the end of a long apprenticeship, this squire is knighted.

How was a squire knighted?

Having completed his apprenticeship, a squire bathed, dressed in a white robe, and spent a night alone in solemn vigil, or prayer. He was then presented with his spurs, shield and sword by an older knight, who gently touched the squire's cheek or neck with his sword.

Why would a squire avoid being knighted?

Becoming a knight was a very expensive business. Some squires preferred to remain as they were, because it was much cheaper.

Why did the Earl of Suffolk knight a French squire?

The Earl was captured by the squire during a battle. Embarrassed to be the prisoner of a mere squire, he knighted the Frenchman.

WINNING HIS SPURS

Receiving his spurs was a sign that a squire had become a knight. Edward III's son, Edward Prince of Wales, became known as the Black Prince when he wore a black surcoat and carried a black shield at the Battle of Crécy in 1357. When asked to help his son in battle, Edward III replied: 'Let the boy win his spurs'.

What was an 'arming doublet'?

A knight wore a leather jacket called an arming doublet, which was covered with laces. These were used to tie on the knight's many pieces of armour.

A knight demonstrates just how agile it is possible to be wearing armour.

Who rode blindly into battle?

The King of Bohemia rode into the Battle of Crécy against the English, but his horse had to be guided by his knights because the king was completely blind.

Could a knight move in his armour?

Yes, although his armour often weighed over 20 kg the weight was evenly spread. Medieval manuscripts describe fully armoured knights turning cartwheels and leaping into the saddle.

How good was a castle's armoury?

An armoury inventory was compiled in 1343, when the Earl of Huntingdon handed over Dover Castle to Sir Bartholomew Burghersh. It lists 50 bows (two generations old); 22 ancient helmets (covered with rotten leather); 25 coats of mail (rusty); 25 antique gauntlets (decayed); 103 shields (34 unserviceable); 6 buckets of arrows (without feathers); 118 lances (18 without heads).

Was it hot in a suit of armour?

It was so hot and difficult to breathe that knights actually died from suffocation in the heat and dust of battle. At the Battle of Agincourt in 1415, many knights, including the Duke of York, suffocated in the mud beneath a huge pile of French bodies.

How was a knight's horse kept peaceful?

A knight's horse wore as much armour as the knight. Some knights also gave their horses wax ear-plugs so that they were not scared by the noise of battle.

Why did priests fight with maces?

The Church prohibited priests from drawing blood with a sword. So many of them used blunt maces instead.

SPACE SUIT

When NASA was designing lightweight, flexible spacesuits for their astronauts, they studied the suit of armour worn in combat by Henry VIII.

How powerful was a longbow?

One Welsh archer fired an arrow from a longbow which passed through a knight's chainmail leggings, his thigh and his saddle, and finally killed his horse.

An archer prepares to let an arrow fly from his longbow.

Why do people stick up two fingers?

This insulting gesture originated with a French threat to chop off the two fingers used by English archers to draw their longbows. When the archers helped to win a great English victory at Agincourt in 1415, they taunted the French by sticking up their two fingers to show that they still had them!

Who wore exploding armour?

At some tournaments knights wore spring-loaded panels of armour during a joust. The armour exploded into fragments if it was successfully struck by the lance of an opponent.

Why did knights wear tokens?

It was considered chivalrous for a knight to perform brave deeds out of a spiritual or 'courtly' love for a lady. Many knights wore tokens of their lady, such as a sleeve or garter, to show their loyalty.

A knight accepts a token of love from his lady.

What was chivalry?

KNIGHT TIME

Before beginning a siege, a chivalrous knight was expected to offer the occupants the chance to surrender and leave unharmed. Sometimes the knight even gave the defenders a set time, such as 30 days, to find help.

Chivalry was a set of rules which outlined the way in which a knight was supposed to behave. According to the laws of chivalry, a knight was expected to be loyal to his lord, to defend the Church, to use his sword to defend widows, orphans and the poor and to be gentle and courteous.

Which king wore a garter?

When the Countess of Salisbury dropped her blue garter, Edward III picked it up and put it on. To celebrate the occasion he formed a society at Windsor Castle for his most chivalrous knights, called the Order of the Garter.

Where did the three lions come from?

The three lions, which are the coat-of-arms of England as well as the badge of the national football team, were first used on the shield of Richard the Lionheart.

Why did a knight wear a turnip?

Canting was a type of heraldry where a knight's coat-of-arms was based on his name. One knight called Rand, which means turnip, proudly decorated his shield with a picture of a turnip.

Who wore a flower-pot on his head?

Knights wore crests on their helmets to show their coat-of-arms. Crests were very elaborate. One Knight of the Garter wore a crest designed to look like a flower-pot with a plant growing from it.

What was the job of a herald?

Heralds kept records of the different coats-of-arms and recorded the deeds of knights during a battle. They also conducted tournaments and kept score in the contests between the knights.

How did a tree of chivalry work?

At tournaments different coloured shields were hung from a 'tree of chivalry'. By touching a shield of a certain colour, the knight's herald selected whichever type of combat his lord wished to fight.

How did heraldry work?

Knights all looked the same covered in armour. So a system of heraldry was developed by which knights could be recognized. It used designs called coats-of-arms, which they wore on their shields, their coats, and the coats of their horses.

When were 2,500 knights held for ransom?

After the Battle of Poitiers in 1356, the victorious English held the French king and 2,500 knights for ransom – according to the rules of chivalry. It cost France a fortune to release them.

This knight has his coat-of-arms on his shield and lance banner, as well as on the horse's coat.

COMMAND OF THE POPES

Popes hoped to prevent tournaments by commanding that any knight killed fighting in one could not receive a Church burial. One knight got round this by changing into a monk's habit before he died from his wounds.

What was a tournament?

It was a pretend battle, in which knights practised their fighting skills. The object was to capture rather than kill your opponent. You could then claim his horse and armour as a prize. Many early tournaments involved a 'mêlée', in which large teams of knights fought each other. Later, the 'joust' became more popular, in which two knights competed by riding at each other with lances.

How many people took part in a tournament?

In early tournaments as many as 3,000 mounted knights would fight in a flat meadow outside a town.

Were tournaments dangerous?

Yes, at one tournament in Cologne 60 knights died. To improve safety knights began using blunt weapons. At Windsor in 1278 the knights wore armour and helmets made from leather, and used swords made from whalebone covered in parchment and silver.

What was the tilt?

The tilt was a barrier first used in the fifteenth century to separate jousting knights. At first it was just a rope, but later a wooden barrier was used. Before the use of the tilt, collisions between jousting knights caused injuries both to knees and horses.

Richly dressed knights joust with one another. Jousting was very dangerous and many knights were fatally injured in tournaments.

Did tournaments always take place on land?

No, one contest took place on the River Thames when it froze over. At other times knights (without their horses) jousted from boats, and on one occasion horses were fitted with horse-shoes made of felt so that a tournament could take place inside a hall.

Who jousted underground?

During the siege of Montereau in 1420, mounted English and French knights jousted by torchlight in the enormous mines the English had dug beneath the French fortifications.

Noble ladies watch the jousting tournament. Many would have been watching for their special knight.

Who wore fancy dress?

Many knights fought at tournaments in fancy dress. At Acre, in Palestine, jousting knights dressed up as nuns, women and characters from the popular story of King Arthur. At Smithfield in 1343, a team of knights dressed up as the Pope and 12 cardinals. One knight even fought wearing the dress of the lady he loved.

WILD GOOSE CHASE

In the People's Crusade of 1096, thousands of peasants marched to the Holy Land behind a preacher called Peter the Hermit and a knight known as Walter the Penniless. Some believed hairs from the tail of Peter the Hermit's donkey were sacred. Others followed a goose, which they said was possessed by the Holy Spirit.

What were the Crusades?

In 1095 Pope Urban II called for Christian knights from Europe to march to the Holy Land on religious 'crusades', or quests, to capture holy cities, such as Jerusalem, from the Muslims. For the next 200 years knights rode off to fight the Crusades. Knights from Europe set up their own kingdoms in the Holy Land, and built enormous castles such as Krak des Chevaliers in Syria.

Which king was never home?

Although he was king of England for ten years, Richard the Lionheart was so busy fighting and crusading that he spent only six months of this time in his own country.

What did Crusaders drink when their water ran out?

In the scorching heat of the desert, Crusaders became trapped in a castle which had no well. They were forced to drink the blood of their horses and their own urine.

Were the Crusaders cannibals?

Yes, some of these Christian warriors did eat human flesh. In 1098 starving Crusaders killed and ate their Muslim prisoners. One of them wrote: 'Our troops boiled pagan adults in cooking pots.'

Who besieged a castle full of sheep?

In 1099 Crusaders besieged a castle defended only by a flock of sheep. The castle garrison had sneaked off during the night, leaving their sheep behind them.

Richard the Lionheart

How did Crusaders give their enemies a buzz?

When the Crusaders were not having much luck firing missiles, dead horses and severed heads from their catapults, they launched bee-hives over the castle walls instead.

Why did old women travel with the Crusaders?

Richard the Lionheart's Crusaders travelled with groups of old women, who cheered them on in battle, washed their bodies and clothes, and picked the lice from their hair.

What did the Crusaders bring back from the Holy Land?

They brought back many new things including chess, playing cards, silk, muslin, carpets, peacocks, windmills, rice, melons, lemons, sugar and wheelbarrows. In 1230 they brought back something less pleasant – leprosy!

Both armies in the Crusades built enormous castles. Crusaders used castles to defend the areas they were trying to recapture from the Muslims.

Who recited poems about knights?

Wandering poets called minstrels or troubadours entertained knights in their castles by reciting poems called romances. These described knights having romantic adventures in which they performed chivalrous deeds and demonstrated 'courtly love'. In this way, the stories set examples that real knights could try to follow.

A troubadour sings and plays the cittern – an early form of guitar.

Who ate her lover's heart?

In the *Châtelain de Coucy*, a famous romance, a dying knight arranges for his last letter and his heart to be sent to the woman he loves. But her husband intercepts the message, cooks the knight's heart and serves it to his wife for dinner!

Who was King Arthur?

Many romances tell the story of King Arthur. Guided by the magician Merlin, Arthur uses an enchanted sword called Excalibur to defeat his enemies. He then gathers together the most chivalrous knights in the land, who become the Knights of the Round Table.

What castle still contains a round table?

A round table from the fourteenth century still hangs in Winchester Castle. It was decorated by Henry VII, who named his own son Arthur.

Where was King Arthur's castle?

According to legend, Arthur built his queen, Guinevere, a beautiful castle called Camelot. Ruins show that the real Camelot may have been at Cadbury Castle in Somerset.

What was courtly love?

Real knights tried to act like the knights in romances by following the ideal of 'courtly love'. They performed brave deeds in the name of a lady who they loved but could never hope to marry – usually because she was already married to somebody else!

Which real king built a round table?

The stories say that King Arthur's knights met at a round table so that no one knight had a better seat than another. When Edward III formed the Order of the Garter around 1350, he also built a round table for his knights to gather around.

Did King Arthur really exist?

The real Arthur was probably a Celtic warrior who lived in the sixth century. Many mothers named their babies Arthur at this time, probably after this man. In medieval times, story-tellers invented romantic stories about Arthur, until he became the king of legend.

Which king dug up Arthur's body?

Edward I dug up a tomb supposed to belong to Arthur and Guinevere at Glastonbury Abbey in 1278, and had the bones reburied in front of his entire court.

How did St George become patron saint of England?

The Crusaders cried out the name of St George in battle, believing the saint could protect them. When Edward III formed the Order of the Garter, St George became its patron saint. Knights wore the red cross on a white background, which was the symbol of St George, and this became the flag of England.

Did St George really kill a dragon?

According to the minstrels' stories, St George was a knight who rescued a king's daughter from a monstrous dragon. But the real St George was probably a Roman soldier who was killed around AD 303 for his Christian beliefs.

St George slays the legendary dragon.

Battles
and Wars

Was William really a conqueror?

William, who came from Normandy in France, became king of England after the Battle of Hastings in 1066. Because he won, William made sure that all the stories about the battle showed him to be a great hero. He became known as William the Conqueror.

Why did William think he should be king of England?

William's cousin, Edward the Confessor, was king of England from 1042 to 1066. William claimed Edward had promised that he could be king after Edward's death.

William and his men survey the newly-conquered nation.

Why didn't the English army face William straight away?

They would have, but they were busy in Yorkshire, fighting someone else. Harald Hardrada (which means 'hard ruler') had invaded from Norway after Edward the Confessor died. Harald was defeated and killed at the Battle of Stamford Bridge on September 25. Three days later William landed on the south coast.

Who wrote the Domesday Book?

William the Conqueror had the Domesday Book written when he was King of England – although William himself couldn't read. It recorded all the land and wealth in the nation.

How did William the Conqueror die?

While fighting the French in his native Normandy in 1087, William's horse stumbled on a hot cinder as the king led a raid in Rouen. As the horse fell, William burst his bladder on the pommel of his saddle and he died shortly afterwards.

During William's reign he had 80 castles built across England.

Why was the battle fought at Hastings?

William and his army had crossed the English Channel from France and landed near Hastings at Pevensey Bay. They camped there for two weeks, built a couple of castles and waited to see if an English army would turn up to force them to return to France.

Did the Normans win the Battle of Hastings easily?

The battle only really started to go the Normans' way when the English leader, Harold, was shot in the eye with an arrow. Harold was a great leader, and without him the English didn't think they could win.

WILLIAM THE STRONG

Stories say that William the Conqueror was so strong he was able to leap on to his horse wearing a full suit of armour. Most knights had to be helped up by their servants (pages).

Who had the biggest army at the Battle of Agincourt?

The English army, under the command of Henry V, had only about 6,000 men, while the French army had 25,000 soldiers.

What was the English army doing in France?

Henry thought he had a claim to the French throne, so he invaded Normandy in August 1415. By September half his men had died in battle or of disease, and he decided to head back to England. He was on his way home when the French army caught up with him.

What happened when the two armies fought?

Amazingly, the French were massacred. They chose a terrible place for the battlefield, because it was just 1 km across. The French soldiers got so jammed in that some of them couldn't even lift their swords. The English archers fired all their arrows, then waded in with swords, hatchets and billhooks. About 1,500 French knights and 4,500 ordinary soldiers died. The English lost about 500 men.

Henry V was known as a pious man and a skilful soldier.

What's a billhook?

A tool or weapon with a curved blade that has a sharp inner edge. Sometimes they could be attached to a long pole, or they might just have a short handle. Billhooks are now generally used for pruning trees and bushes.

Why did the English boil their dead?

They didn't boil all of them, just two. The Earl of Oxford and the Duke of York were both killed. Henry didn't want to leave them in France, but he knew their bodies would rot if they were carried home. So he had them boiled until the flesh dropped off and took the skeletons home.

What happened to the prisoners?

The English took a lot of French prisoners early in the battle, and Henry had them sent to the rear of the soldiers. But then the French attacked again from in front. Henry thought the prisoners might try to attack him from behind, so he had them all killed.

Who had sent Henry a present of tennis balls?

The king of France. France and England had been at war for years (the war eventually became known as the Hundred Years' War). The message of the tennis balls was meant to be: 'Stay at home and play tennis. It will be better for you than coming to France.'

Why were England and France at war for 100 years?

The Hundred Years' War actually went on for 116 years. It started in 1337 and ended in 1453. The fighting was over who should be king of France. The kings of England thought they should rule France as well. By the time Henry V died, England controlled all of France north of the river Loire, including Paris.

TENNIS-LOVING MONARCHS

Henry was sent tennis balls by the French king as an insult. But some English monarchs actually liked playing tennis. Henry VIII was playing tennis when his wife, Anne Boleyn, was executed. The best royal tennis player was George VI, who played at Wimbledon in the 1920's and won a trophy.

Joan of Arc is burnt at the stake for being a witch, despite her bravery against the English during the battle at Orleans.

Who was Joan of Arc?

Joan of Arc was a big problem for the English. She led a French army that drove them away from the city of Orleans, which proved a turning point in the Hundred Years' War. From then on the English controlled less and less of France.

English warships were cramped, dark and unhygienic places to live.

How did the English defeat the Armada?

Strictly speaking, they didn't. The Spanish made it to Calais without losing many ships. Then the English sent fireships into the harbour and the Spanish panicked. At the Battle of Gravelines, the English sank one Spanish ship and scattered the rest. But what really did the damage was a great storm that blew the Spanish into the North Sea.

A SAILOR'S LIFE

Conditions in the English fleet were terrible. The sailors who fought against the Armada in July and August still hadn't been paid in September. Some even died of starvation because they couldn't afford to eat.

Which commander played bowls as the Spanish invaders arrived?

Legend has it that Sir Francis Drake finished a game of bowls he was playing before setting off to sea to fight the Spanish invasion fleet in 1588. Drake was one of England's greatest sea captains.

Why did the Spanish want to invade England?

King Philip of Spain wanted to invade England because it was a Protestant country, while he was a Catholic, and because England was supporting a revolt against Spanish rule in the Netherlands. The Spanish fleet – called the Armada – was on its way to Flanders. Once there, it was to have helped ferry 30,000 Spanish troops across the English Channel to invade England.

Who had the best ships, the English or the Spanish?

The Spanish had larger ships which could carry many men – up to 27,000 men were crammed into their 130 ships. The English had smaller, faster-moving ships which carried far greater numbers of cannon, and English gunners were usually very accurate.

Was the Spanish attack a surprise?

English spies had discovered the plan to invade, and the Armada was attacked before it had even left Spain. Then, when it tried to leave again, it was forced back to port by a great storm. The Spanish finally arrived in the English Channel in July 1588, just as Drake was finishing his game of bowls.

Why were the Spanish especially keen to fight Drake?

Sir Francis had spent most of the years 1585 and 1586 in the Caribbean, capturing Spanish ships and stealing their treasure. The Spanish claimed he was a pirate, but to most English people he was a hero. Queen Elizabeth I loved him too, because he kept sending her Spanish gold.

As the Spanish fled to safety, many of their ships were wrecked on rocks or sandbanks off the coast.

SIR WALTER RALEIGH

Raleigh was a famous Elizabethan sailor and explorer and he was a great favourite of Queen Elizabeth I. Stories say that he once laid his cloak across a puddle for the Queen so that she wouldn't get her feet wet. Unfortunately, this story isn't true. People also claim that Sir Walter brought potatoes and tobacco back to Europe from the New World. Unfortunately, this isn't true either, though he did try to found a colony in North America and sailed to South America in search of gold.

How many Spanish ships made it back to Spain?

Of the 130 ships that set out, about 60 made it home. The rest had been wrecked in storms or sunk by the English. It took them so long to get home (over two months) that many of the men on board had died of starvation.

Which king lost his head?

Charles I, who got into an argument with Parliament and ended up being beheaded. He had summoned Parliament to help him pay for a war with Scotland, but then the parliamentarians wouldn't go away again. Eventually there was a war between the Royalists ('Cavaliers') and the Parliamentarians ('Roundheads').

CHARLES I'S NECK-BONE

The neck-bone that had been chopped through by Charles I's executioner was later used by Sir Henry Halford, as a salt shaker.

How did the Roundheads get their name?

It was from the shape of their helmets, which were round with a slight lip around the edge. They were worn by Oliver Cromwell's New Model Army.

Who was Oliver Cromwell?

Cromwell was a member of Parliament who became a successful general. He led the Roundhead forces at the Battle of Naseby in 1645, where the king's army was destroyed. Later, the king was captured, but he escaped to Scotland and tried to invade England from there. Cromwell defeated him again, at the Battle of Preston in 1648, and Charles fell into Parliament's hands once more.

What was the Rump Parliament?

The Rump Parliament was the group of Members of Parliament that was most committed to executing the king. After his death, they declared England a Commonwealth. After Cromwell and his Roundhead army had put down revolts in Scotland and Ireland, the whole of Britain became part of the Commonwealth. Cromwell was now the most powerful man in Britain.

What disease was a king's touch supposed to cure?

Scrofula, which was common when Charles II was on the throne. People used to line up to be touched by him in the hope of being cured. Unfortunately, there's no evidence that it worked. Six people were once killed when the queue they were in rushed forward and they were crushed.

Who was Lord Protector of the Commonwealth?

Oliver Cromwell, who had been a great opponent of the king's right to govern alone, became ruler in December 1653. He ruled until his death in 1658.

Why did the king wear two shirts to his execution?

He was worried he'd shiver in the cold January air and the crowds that had gathered to watch the execution would think he was scared. Charles had written his last words on a sheet of paper so that he wouldn't forget them. But in the end he said them in a whisper and no one heard.

Who decided to execute the king?

Parliament, but only just. In fact, the decision to execute Charles was made by just one vote.

Who was the 'Merry Monarch'?

Charles II, who became king two years after Cromwell's death. He was the son of Charles I and had fought for him during the Civil War when the Roundheads fought the Cavaliers. He was said to have escaped capture by the Roundheads on one occasion by spending days hiding up a tree.

Charles II, the first king after the Royalists regained power, hides from Cromwell's army up a tree.

Paul Revere rides to warn the Minutemen that the British forces are approaching.

Which tea party started a war?

The American War of Independence, also called the American Revolution, began in 1775. America was an British colony at the time. To protest about the amount of taxes they had to pay to the British government, a group of Americans dressed up as Native Americans and dumped a load of tea into Boston Harbour in 1773. This became known as the Boston Tea Party.

THE MAD KING?

George III, who was king of Britain during the American War of Independence, went through periods when he seemed mad. He once told his courtiers that he was going to adopt a new son, named Octavius. They were surprised to discover that Octavius was, in fact, a pillow.

Who was Paul Revere?

One of the people who had dressed up as a Native American for the Boston Tea Party. He later became famous for riding to warn the Minutemen (American patriots) of the approach of British forces. His warning meant that the Minutemen were ready the next morning to fight a battle at Lexington Green. This battle started the War of Independence.

Why did the Americans dress up as Native Americans?

It was meant to be a disguise. The protesters didn't want to be put in prison or executed, so they pretended to be Native Americans. They thought no one would notice that they were actually white men.

Who were the Minutemen?

A group of Americans who were trained to be ready at a minute's warning to fight the British. They were guerillas who knew the country far better than the British troops. The British found them very difficult to fight, because the Minutemen didn't behave like an ordinary army. They usually appeared, shot a few soldiers, then disappeared again.

What did General Cornwallis get for Christmas?

A nasty surprise. Cornwallis was a British general who had driven the American rebel forces back across the river Delaware by December 1776. On Christmas night, the American General Washington recrossed the Delaware and attacked Cornwallis. He took 1,000 British soldiers prisoner.

Who were 'George's friends'?

A group of people in England who were close to King George III. They advised him to take a harsh line with the American rebels, instead of trying to reach an agreement with them. In the end, the advice of George's friends lost him all his territories south of the Canadian border.

Who helped the Americans?

A German soldier named Baron Friedrich von Steuben gave American troops important training in the winter of 1777–1778. But the most important foreign helpers were the French, who supported the revolution all along, and actually declared war on England in June 1778.

Who became king of America?

No one. The Americans didn't want a king, even though almost everyone else had one. Instead, they voted for a president. The first one was George Washington, who had been one of their best generals. They decided to vote for the president every four years.

George Washington – a brilliant military commander.
He was elected first US president in April 1789.

THE VICTORY

Admiral Lord Nelson's warship, HMS *Victory*, was launched in 1765, making her 40 years old at the Battle of Trafalgar. After bringing Admiral Nelson's body home, she sailed back to carry on the fight against Napoleon Bonaparte. The *Victory* is now in dry dock in Portsmouth, England.

What was a cat o' nine tails?

A special whip with nine separate strands of leather. It was used to punish sailors who had broken the ship's rules. After he had been flogged, salt was rubbed into a man's back to stop the wound from getting infected.

Who is said to have asked to be kissed on his deathbed?

Admiral Lord Nelson, the hero of the British Navy. He had just been shot and realised he was about to die. Legend has it that he said 'Kiss me, Hardy'. Hardy was one of his officers, and was holding Nelson in his arms. Actually, Nelson's last words were 'Thank God I have done my duty.'

Which admiral couldn't see a signal visible to everyone else?

An old injury made Nelson blind in one eye. At the Battle of Copenhagen in 1801, Nelson's commanding officer ordered him to withdraw, thinking the battle was lost. Nelson placed his telescope to his blind eye and claimed not to be able to see the signal, then carried on to win the battle.

How did Nelson come to be shot at Trafalgar?

Nelson was leading the British Navy against a larger French fleet at Trafalgar, in 1805. The British fleet had been sent to attack the French and protect England from the invasion which Napoleon was said to be planning. Nelson divided his fleet in two and they attacked the French fleet. Nelson's ship, HMS *Victory*, was in a skirmish with two French warships and he was shot by a sniper during a battle with the French ship *Redoutable*.

What was life like in the British Navy?

Life was very tough for ordinary sailors. The work was hard, the food was terrible and there wasn't enough space. Only the captain had his own cabin, and on most ships even that wasn't much bigger than a cupboard. Discipline was strict and anyone who broke the ship's rules was severely punished. Men could be flogged (whipped) with a cat o' nine tails, or even hanged.

What happened when Nelson died?

The nation went into mourning. He was England's greatest naval commander, and had twice stopped Napoleon Bonaparte from invading Britain. To honour his memory, a huge column was erected in London. The column is called Nelson's Column and it still stands in Trafalgar Square today.

Who won the Battle of Trafalgar?

Nelson had 27 ships and the French had 33. He split his force in two and attacked both ends of the French line of ships. When the battle was at its most fierce, Nelson raised a famous signal: 'England expects that every man will do his duty'. The French were cut to pieces in the fighting that followed. They lost 20 ships and about 14,000 men. The British lost about 1,500 men, including Nelson, but no ships.

Did many people want to join the Navy?

Plenty of young men wanted to be officers, but very few ordinary sailors wanted to join the Navy. Many were forced to join by 'press gangs', which were sent ashore to kidnap men who were then forced to work on the ships.

Ships battle it out at Trafalgar while Nelson lies dying.

Napoleon, brooding on the island of Elba, plans for his return to power.

Which French leader returned to fight another day?

Napoleon Bonaparte, who had been ruler of France (and most of Europe) from 1804 to 1814. He was finally defeated in April 1814 and exiled to the Mediterranean island of Elba. But Napoleon escaped and returned to France in 1815.

How did the French react to Napoleon's return?

Many people were delighted, and lots of Napoleon's old soldiers rejoined his army. In the rest of Europe they weren't so pleased. Austria, Britain, Prussia and Russia decided to send an army to defeat the French. Napoleon's spies told him of the plan and he led an army to attack the allied force. The armies met at a place called Waterloo.

Were many people killed at the Battle of Waterloo?

The fighting lasted from June 15 to 18. It was one of the bloodiest battles in history. On the last day alone, 40,000 French soldiers and 22,000 allied soldiers were killed. At one point about 45,000 men were lying dead or wounded within an area of 8 square kilometres.

What was the Old Guard?

Napoleon's best troops and his personal bodyguards. They were kept in reserve to be used only when they were most badly needed.

GEORGE IV AND THE BIG LIE

King George IV was a terrible liar. Even though he was so fat he could barely sit on a horse, he used to tell people that he had led a cavalry charge at the Battle of Waterloo. 'Isn't that true, Wellington?' he asked one of his star generals. The duke's clever reply was: 'I have often heard you say so, your majesty.'

Who won the Battle of Waterloo?

The allies, although for much of the fighting it was impossible to tell who was likely to win. Mistakes by two of Napoleon's commanders and Wellington's clever tactics meant that in the end Napoleon was being attacked from so many sides he was defeated. He only escaped thanks to the bravery of the Old Guard.

Was Napoleon banished to Elba again?

No, he was captured by the allies and sent to live on the island of St Helena, right in the middle of the Atlantic Ocean. It was so far away that it would be impossible for him to return to France in secret and start yet another war.

Who led the allied army at Waterloo?

General Arthur Wellesley, the Duke of Wellington. He had already successfully defeated Napoleon's forces during the Peninsula War where Wellington's armies had forced the French out of Spain.

Wellington and his commanders survey the battlefield at Waterloo.

Which Nightingale worked at the Battle of Balaklava?

The nurse Florence Nightingale brought aid to the wounded after the battle, which was during the Crimean War in 1854, in what is now Russia. She had heard reports of the terrible conditions the soldiers endured and volunteered to take 38 nurses with her to help those injured in battle.

Florence Nightingale tends wounded soldiers at Scutari hospital during the Crimean War.

What happened to Florence Nightingale after the war?

She returned to England in 1860, as the war finished. The public donated money with which she started Britain's first school for nurses, at St Thomas' Hospital in London.

Which General wasn't sure who he was fighting?

Lord Raglan, the British commander, was 67 years old and a bit senile. Raglan had fought against France during the Napoleonic wars 40 years earlier, and he insisted on calling the enemy 'the French', even though the French were actually on his side.

What was the Charge of the Light Brigade?

The Light Brigade was a unit of cavalry in the British Army. They were ordered to charge along a valley to attack a Russian position, but almost all were killed by the Russian guns. The poet Alfred Tennyson wrote a famous poem about what heroes the men of the Light Brigade were.

What was it like being a soldier in the Crimean War?

Life was terrible for the ordinary soldiers. They rarely had enough to eat, and during the winter they shivered in the cold air. In summertime, many soldiers died of dysentery, because there were very few proper toilets and the water supplies became contaminated. More soldiers died of sickness than of battle injuries.

Did the soldiers protest about the conditions?

Not if they had any sense. The British Army still allowed soldiers to be flogged (whipped) if their commanding officer thought it right. All other European countries had stopped this by the time the British finally gave it up in 1881.

THE CHARGE OF THE LIGHT BRIGADE – STUPID OR BRAVE?

The Charge of the Light Brigade became a famous poem by Alfred Tennyson, which asked 'When can their glory fade? Oh, the wild charge they made!' A French general named Bosquet, who watched the charge, had a slightly different view: 'It's magnificent, but it isn't war – it's stupidity.'

Soldiers line up in readiness for the Charge of the Light Brigade.

How did people at home find out about the war?

Through journalists. The Crimean War was the first war in which journalists accompanied the soldiers and witnessed the fighting. They sent back reports of the terrible conditions that shocked people at home and led to pressure on the government to end the war quickly.

Zulu warriors were famed for their bravery and ferocity.

Who cleaned their spears on the tunics of English soldiers?

The Zulu warriors of Cetshwayo, in 1879. The Zulus won a huge battle against the British Army, at a place called Ishandlwana. They called this great battle 'The Washing Of The Spears', because so much blood was shed.

Who was Shaka Zulu?

The great warrior-leader of the Zulu people, who died in 1828. He had built the Zulu empire up from a small territory to a huge nation with a large, efficient army. By the time Cetshwayo became leader, the Zulus controlled over 50,000 square kilometres of southern Africa, and their empire was growing.

What was the Battle of Rorke's Drift?

One hundred and thirty-nine soldiers defended the base against an army of 4,000 warriors. Eleven Victoria Crosses were awarded to soldiers who fought at Rorke's Drift. The Victoria Cross is the highest honour a British soldier can get.

MFECANE – 'THE CRUSHING'

During the early 1800s the Zulu empire was expanding. The British had established bases at Durban and Cape Town, and the Dutch had trekked north in covered wagons searching for farmland. Several peoples were squeezed out by the newcomers, and found new homes as far away as Zimbabwe, Mozambique and Zambia. The Zulus called this process *mfecane* – which means 'the crushing'.

Why were the British fighting the Zulus?

They wanted the same land as the Zulus. Southern Africa had rich farmland and, even better, gold and diamonds had been discovered there. To get control of the area the British sent 5,000 European and 10,000 African soldiers into Zulu territory.

How did Zulus armed with spears beat soldiers with rifles and machine guns?

The Zulus sprung a neat trap on the British. About 2,000 British troops were camped at a place called Ishandlwana. They spotted a small group of Zulus in the distance and some men were sent after them. As the pursuers chased the Zulus over a crest, they stopped dead in their tracks. Below them was crouched an army of 20,000 Zulu warriors.

How many soldiers died at Ishandlwana?

About 1,400 men were massacred. The rest fled – some were killed later by the Zulus, others found their way to a place called Rorke's Drift. This was a British base on the Buffalo river.

What was an *assegai*?

A Zulu spear, which was used together with a long shield for hand-to-hand fighting. It had a long, broad blade and a fairly short handle, and could be used for stabbing or throwing.

A British soldier with a bayonet faces a Zulu warrior with a spear.

The Mahdi or 'divinely guided one' intended to banish the Anglo-Egyptian forces from the Sudan.

What earned Gordon the name Chinese Gordon?

He had fought in the 'Arrow War' in China, and was there when the British occupied Peking (now called Beijing). Gordon got the job of burning down the Chinese emperor's summer palace, as a way of teaching him a lesson for defying the British.

What was the Ever-Victorious Army?

A group of Chinese peasants led by Gordon, who defended the European trading city of Shanghai against attack during the Taiping Rebellion. Gordon led the Ever-Victorious Army for 18 months, until the rebellion had been crushed. It was never defeated and he returned to England a hero.

Why was a British general made governor of the Sudan?

Because the ruler of Egypt, who was called the Khedive, was kept in power by the British. He often employed British officers, and when he needed a new governor of Sudan, Gordon got the job. Gordon was already a hero in Britain following his bravery in the Crimean War and China.

What was the Siege of Khartoum?

When he arrived in Khartoum, the capital of Sudan, Gordon's aim was to evacuate the city before the Mahdi arrived. He knew he couldn't win a battle with his much smaller forces. Two thousand women, children and sick people were evacuated, but then the Mahdi's army arrived in March 1884. They put Khartoum under siege, and it stayed under siege for almost a year.

Who made the Mahdi mad?

The British general Charles Gordon, who was also known as Chinese Gordon. The Mahdi was the leader of a group of Sudanese fighters who wanted to take control of their country away from the Egyptians. Gordon had been appointed governor-general of Sudan by the Egyptian ruler.

Did the British send an army to help Gordon?

Not at first. The prime minister, William Gladstone, had only reluctantly agreed to let Gordon go to Sudan, and he didn't want to send anyone to help. But by August, Gladstone was forced to act on pressure from the public and Queen Victoria.

Was Khartoum saved?

No. The relief army arrived too late. The Mahdi had been about to call off the siege when the level of the Nile, which flowed past the city, dropped. A gap in the battlements opened, and the Mahdi's forces made one last attack and broke into the city. The relief army arrived two days later.

What happened to the people of Khartoum?

Most of them were massacred. The Mahdi had been going to have Khartoum as his capital, but the smell of dead bodies was so bad that he had to move to the nearby city of Omdurman.

GLADSTONE

The slow speed with which William Gladstone sent help to Gordon cost him dear. It was so unpopular a decision with the British public that it was part of the reason for him losing the next election!

What happened to Chinese Gordon?

The Mahdi had expressly said that he did not want Gordon to be killed if Khartoum was captured. Unfortunately, the attackers didn't take any notice of this command. Gordon was slaughtered with the rest of the city's defenders.

Gordon awaits certain death in Khartoum.

Which 'lions' were led by 'donkeys'?

British soldiers during the First World War (1914–1918). Although the soldiers were famously brave, their generals were also famously stupid. A German officer once compared the British Army with lions (the soldiers) being led by donkeys (the generals).

OVER THE TOP

The soldiers called the moment when they had to climb out of their trenches and attack 'going over the top'. It was so dangerous that they often wrote farewell letters to their families before an attack. One soldier wrote to his wife: 'We are going over the top this afternoon and only God in Heaven knows who will come out alive'.

Life in the trenches was horrific for the soldiers. They suffered from cold, lack of clean water, disease and hunger.

Why were the British generals stupid?

They had expected the war to be over quickly, but when the armies met, neither could get the upper hand. Instead, they dug in along what became known as the Western Front.

What was a war of attrition?

The idea was that if you had a battle where you lost 10,000 men and the enemy lost 12,000 men, you had won the battle even if no one had gained any territory. Eventually, the enemy would run out of soldiers, and the war would be over. The generals stuck with this idea for several years.

What was the worst battle?

For the British, the bloodiest battle was the Somme (July–September 1916). The greatest number of British soldiers ever killed in a battle died there. 20,000 soldiers died and 60,000 were injured on the first day alone.

How many shells were fired at the Battle of the Somme?

During the 'softening-up' attack on the German trenches, 1,700,000 shells were fired over a period of eight days. No one is sure exactly how many shells were fired during the whole battle.

What new weapon did the British use?

Tanks were used for the first time at the Somme. They weren't very successful – half of them failed even to start, and others broke down in no-man's land (the land between the two sides). But people began to see how they could be very useful in a battle.

Was the Somme the worst battle of the war?

Possibly not. At the Battle of Passchendaele (July–Nov 1917) over 24,000 men died on the first day. The poet Siegfried Sassoon wrote: 'I died in hell – they called it Passchendaele'. For the French army, the Battle of Verdun (Feb–Dec 1916) was the worst – over 500,000 men died.

What was no-man's land?

The space between the opposing trenches. Often it was quite narrow and, at Christmas, the soldiers could hear the other side singing carols. No-man's land was filled with bomb craters, barbed wire, mines and dead bodies.

How many men died at the Somme?

In total, over 1,000 000 men were killed. When it was over, the Allies had won a strip of land approximately 35 kilometres long and 19 kilometres wide. Over 3,000 men died for each square kilometre.

British troops attacking a German trench.

The Spitfire was one of the most successful planes during the Second World War.

What kind of planes took part in the Battle of Britain?

On the British side, Hurricanes and Spitfires. The Germans had Messerschmidt fighters and Heinkel bombers. The Spitfire was the plane the Luftwaffe pilots feared most: it was fast and manoeuvrable.

What nationality were the RAF pilots?

Most were British, but there were pilots from elsewhere too. There were Poles and Czechs, among others, who had escaped when their countries were overrun by the Germans.

Were the British well prepared for the Battle of Britain?

In June 1940, a month before the Battle of Britain began, the chief of Fighter Command told the government that if the Germans attacked he wouldn't be able to keep air superiority for more than 24 hours. But by the time the battle started, 715 planes were available, with 424 ready to be built.

What was the Battle of Britain?

From July to September 1940 the Luftwaffe (German air force) tried to get control of the skies over the English Channel and southern England. The air battles between the RAF and the Luftwaffe became known as the Battle of Britain.

Why did the Germans stop using Stukas?

The Germans did use their Stuka dive-bomber planes at first, but on August 18, 1940, 87 Stukas were shot down. The Germans only used them again on very rare occasions.

THE FINAL DAY

The Battle of Britain effectively ended on September 15, 1940. In a day of heavy fighting Fighter Command shot down over 60 Luftwaffe planes. The Germans realised that they would not be able to control the skies over the Channel, and shelved their plans to invade Britain.

THE BLITZ

The Blitz – a series of heavy bombing raids on London – began on September 7, 1940. The Luftwaffe thought that it could force Fighter Command to defend London in large numbers, which would give the opportunity to shoot down more British fighters. The RAF had also bombed Berlin, which made Hitler so furious that he decided to switch his attacks to London.

What was a 'scramble'?

When Fighter Command got warning of approaching German planes they telephoned through to the airfield. When the phone rang and the order 'Scramble!' was given, the pilots dropped everything and climbed into their planes.

Who kept score during the Battle of Britain?

Every day the newspapers carried headlines like 'Luftwaffe 10, RAF 124'. The numbers of German planes shot down were rarely as high as claimed, but during two of the heaviest days of fighting – August 15 and 16, 1940 – two Luftwaffe planes were shot down for every RAF plane. By late August, the Luftwaffe had lost over 600 aircraft while the RAF had lost just 260.

Which pilots stopped a Sealion invading Britain?

The pilots of Fighter Command, part of the Royal Air Force (RAF). The Germans wanted to invade Britain during the Second World War – the invasion was codenamed Operation Sealion. But they needed control of the skies, which meant that they had to beat the RAF.

RAF pilots get ready to take off whilst under fire from German bombers.

General Bernard Montgomery

General Erwin Rommel

Who was Monty?

Monty was the nickname of the British commander of the 8th Army in Africa, General Bernard Montgomery. After leading the defeat of Rommel at the Battle of El Alamein, he went on to command the British and Canadian forces on D-Day.

Who were the Desert Rats?

The Desert Rats was the nickname of the 7th Armoured Division of the British Army. They were first called rats by the Nazi radio broadcaster Lord Haw-Haw, as an insult. But they liked the name so much that they decided to keep it.

Who was the Desert Fox?

The German general, Erwin Rommel. He was called the Desert Fox by both the British and the Germans, because of his cunning surprise attacks. He was so successful that Hitler quickly promoted him to Field Marshal.

What was the Battle of El Alamein?

Rommel was ordered by Hitler to attack the British in Cairo, their main base in North Africa. He was stopped within 100 kilometres of the city, at a place called El Alamein, in 1942. Although the British were pleased, many Arabs were disappointed: they saw Rommel as a liberator who would free them from the British.

How did Rommel almost become the ruler of Germany?

In 1944 some of Rommel's friends suggested that if Hitler were overthrown he should become the German leader. Unknown to Rommel, these same friends were plotting to assassinate Hitler. But Hitler survived, and Rommel was arrested. He took poison in prison and died, to save his family from punishment.

What was the Battle of Tobruk?

Tobruk was the last city in North Africa unconquered by the Africa Korps, Rommel's army. It was guarded by the 9th Australian Division. If Tobruk had been captured, the Germans might have been able to attack the British in Egypt.

LORD HAW-HAW

Lord Haw-Haw was an Englishman who supported Hitler and went to live in Germany. He sent radio broadcasts to Britain saying that Germany was about to win the war and that Britain should surrender. His real name was William Joyce, but his 'posh' accent was so ridiculous that people called him Lord Haw-Haw.

How did Hitler survive being assassinated?

By sheer luck he was shielded from the force of the bomb that went off in his command centre.

Towards the end of the battle at El Alamein, the Germans had only 90 tanks against the Allied forces' 800.

The *Graf Spee* explodes having been scuttled by her commander.

Why did a German commander sink his own ship?

He thought (wrongly) that there was a powerful British fleet waiting for him just over the horizon. Hitler ordered him not to surrender because the ship would then be captured by the British. The only other option was to sink the ship.

What's a pocket battleship?

After losing the First World War Germany was forbidden to build full-sized battleships. Instead, they built pocket battleships – smaller, well-armed versions.

Who served up their battleship on a plate?

The German Navy. The pocket battleship *Graf Spee* was scuttled (deliberately sunk) by her commander near the mouth of the River Plate in Uruguay, in December 1939.

How did the Royal Navy find the *Graf Spee*?

A merchant ship managed to send out a signal 'R-R-R', indicating an attack by a raider, before she was sunk. Three ships, HMS *Exeter*, HMS *Ajax* and HMNZS *Achilles*, set off in pursuit. After the Battle of the River Plate, the three ships managed to chase the *Graf Spee* into Montevideo harbour.

SNORKELLING SUBMARINES!

Near to the end of the war, German U-boats were fitted with a device called a snorkel. This allowed them to stay below the surface for long periods, but it came too late to save Germany from defeat.

How successful was the Bismarck?

In her first battle, the *Bismarck* sank HMS *Hood*, a British battle cruiser sent to intercept it. But the Royal Navy was closing in on the *Bismarck* – almost the entire Home Fleet had set off in pursuit. The *Bismarck*'s steering gear was wrecked by torpedo planes, and she could only turn in a large circle. Within a few hours the British had caught up.

How many U-boats did the Royal Navy destroy?

Germany built 1,162 U-boats, of which 785 were destroyed or captured. Of these 41 were destroyed in the month of May 1943 alone. After this, the wolf packs were never such a dangerous threat to Allied shipping.

Which was the most powerful German battleship ever?

The *Bismarck*, which joined the German Navy in August 1940. She had eight 15-inch guns and twelve 5.9-inch guns, as well as numerous other weapons.

How was the Bismarck sunk?

With a combination of torpedoes and gunfire from British battleships. The *Bismarck*'s crew realised their ship was a flaming wreck and set off explosions inside the hull. Within a short time the *Bismarck* had sunk.

What were the wolf packs?

Groups of German submarines (called U-boats) which attacked Allied ships during the Battle of the Atlantic. They waited in a line across the shipping lanes until one of the U-boats spotted a convoy of ships. A radio message called the other subs, and when enough had gathered, they launched an attack on the convoy.

A U-boat comes to the surface having torpedoed an Allied ship.

Heroes and
Villains

What was the Gunpowder Plot?

The Gunpowder Plot was an attempt by a group of Catholics to blow up the Houses of Parliament in 1605. On November 5 one of the plotters, Guy Fawkes, was discovered leaving Parliament's cellars. Hidden in his pockets were fuses for lighting explosives and behind him in the cellar were 36 barrels of gunpowder.

INSTRUMENTS OF TORTURE

Guy Fawkes was tortured on a rack. This was a device that stretched the body until the pain was unbearable. After several days of being stretched on the rack, Guy was forced to give up his secrets.

Who was Guy Fawkes?

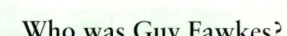

Guy Fawkes was a member of the Catholic religion at a time when members of the Catholic and Protestant religions hated one another. The Gunpowder Plot was a protest against anti-Catholic laws brought in by King James I.

Why did the plotters choose November 5?

It was the day Parliament opened – the House of Lords, the House of Commons and King James I were all going to be there. The plotters hoped to blow up as many of them as possible.

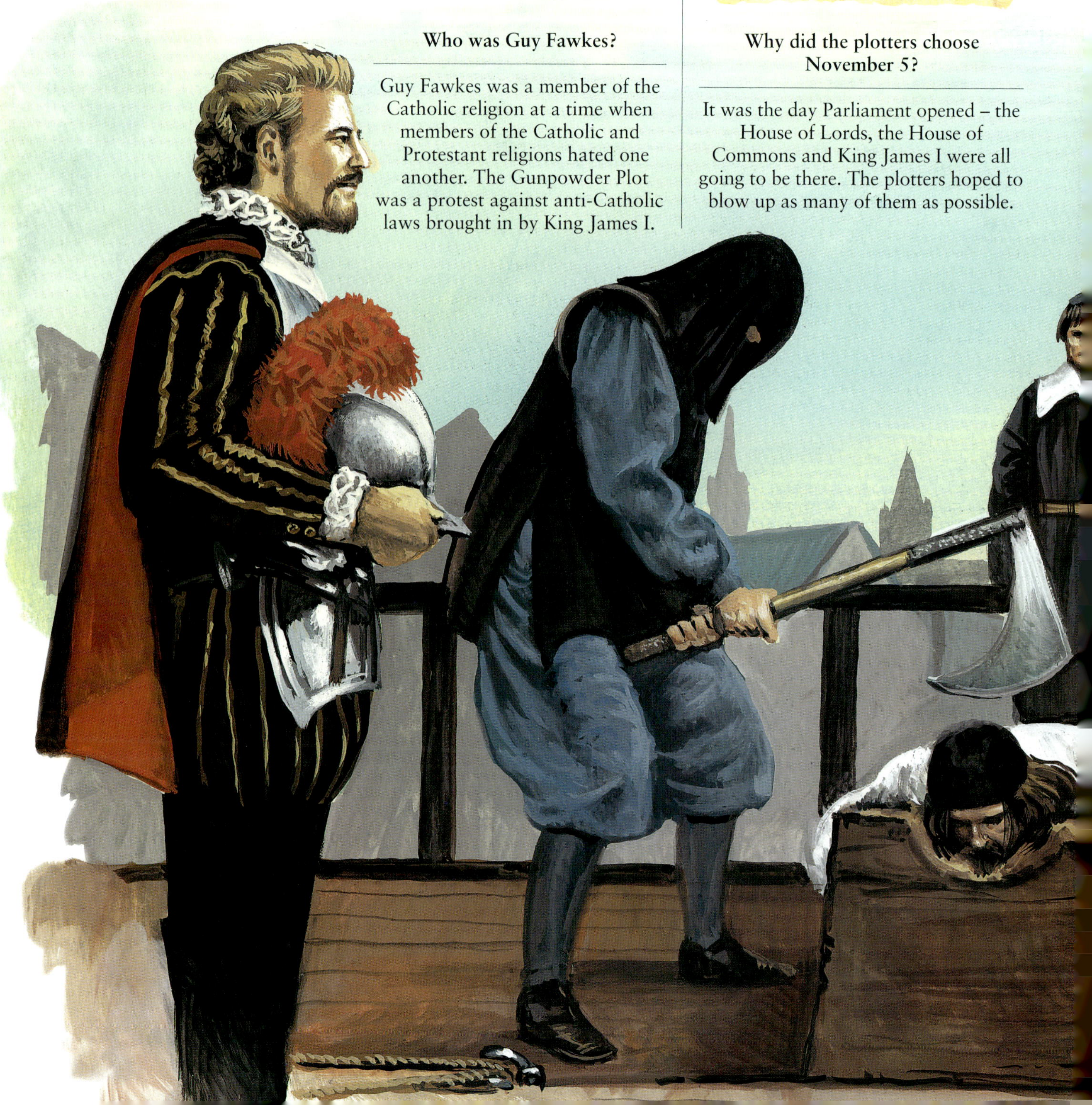

How was the Gunpowder Plot discovered?

One of the plotters wrote to a friend of his who was a member of the House of Lords, warning him not to go to the opening of Parliament that day. The authorities were alerted and they then discovered Guy Fawkes and the barrels of gunpowder.

How were the rest of the conspirators found out?

Guy was tortured, which was a common way of getting information from people in those days. It took a long time to force him to confess, but in the end he gave up the names of the other plotters.

Only nobles were usually executed on the block. Guy Fawkes and his fellow-plotters suffered the horrible traitors death of being hung, drawn and quartered.

Lord Haw-Haw

Who was Lord Haw-Haw?

Lord Haw-Haw was a famous British traitor – although he was actually born in the USA. His real name was William Joyce. During the Second World War (1939–45) he worked for the Nazis, broadcasting Nazi radio propaganda to Britain.

What happened to Lord Haw-Haw at the end of the war?

Lord Haw-Haw was captured by the Allies. Because he held a British passport he was taken to Britain, where he was convicted of treason and hanged.

Why did the British call William Joyce 'Lord Haw-Haw'?

Because he put on a ridiculous British upper-class accent. People thought it was so stupid they started calling him Lord Haw-Haw.

Who were Britain's worst modern-day traitors?

A group of spies who passed secrets to the Soviet Union. Guy Burgess and Donald Maclean were discovered and fled to Moscow in 1951. Kim Philby followed in 1963, and in 1979 Anthony Blunt was revealed as the fourth spy.

Did Robin Hood really exist?

Some people think Robin Hood may have been a real person named Robert Fitzooth, the Earl of Huntington. But there are many versions of the story of Robin Hood, so he may have been based on a number of different people.

When did Robin Hood live?

The earliest versions of his story come from the 1300s. But most stories about Robin suggest that he was an outlaw during the rule of Richard the Lionheart, from 1189 to1199.

Why was Robin Hood an outlaw?

In most versions of the story, Robin is a Saxon nobleman. He became an outlaw to fight the Normans who invaded Britain with William the Conqueror in 1066. The Normans forced the people to pay heavy taxes, which went towards making the Normans rich and the people of England even poorer.

Why was he called Robin Hood?

Robin was supposed to be so skilled at archery that he could hit a target while his hood was pulled down to cover his eyes. But Robin's main activity was robbing rich Normans who strayed into his part of Sherwood Forest. He then gave the money to the poor folk who lived nearby.

Who was Robin's main enemy?

The Sheriff of Nottingham. The Sheriff was based in a large castle the Normans had built at Nottingham.

Who is known as the 'Scottish Robin Hood'?

Rob Roy (whose real name was Robert Macgregor). He was a cattle dealer whose lands were taken away from him by the Duke of Montrose. Rob Roy became a Scottish hero for fighting against such a large landowner.

Robin Hood and his band of outlaws.

Was Richard's family as popular as he was?

Not really: there were all sorts of rumours about Richard the Lionheart's family, and people said that they were in league with the devil. One story told that Richard's ancestor, the Count of Anjou, married a demon from Hell disguised as a beautiful woman. Her descendants all had the Devil's blood running through their veins. It was even said that Richard's brother, John, was a werewolf!

What were the Crusades?

The Crusades were a set of wars fought in the Holy Lands (which are now the countries of Lebanon and Israel). Knights and noblemen from Europe went there to try and capture the land where the Christian religion began.

What kinds of weapons did people have then?

Knights on the Crusades generally fought with swords, though they could also ride horses and use a lance. Some used a mace, a thick stick with a heavy chain attached. At the end of the chain was a large spiked ball, which was swung at the enemy and could inflict terrible injuries. Ordinary soldiers used swords, pikes, bows and arrows and crossbows.

RUTHLESS RICHARD

At the siege of Acre, Richard the Lionheart's forces took 2,700 Muslim prisoners. Then he ordered his men to slaughter every single one of them. Richard was buried near his father at Fontevraud in France. But his heart was buried miles away in the city of Rouen!

King Richard was a heroic soldier, but during his reign the people of England suffered great poverty.

Why was Richard called 'The Lionheart'?

King Richard was a hero in England because he was a great fighter. However, he spent much of his time as king away in the Holy Lands, on a Crusade fighting Muslim armies.

Who was the most bloodthirsty of the pirates?

The most famous and most feared pirate was Edward Teach – otherwise known as Blackbeard. For two years from 1716 to 1718 he plundered the coast of the south-eastern America. To make himself look even more terrifying, Blackbeard used to put lighted cords of tar into his hair before he went into battle.

How did pirates capture the ships of their victims?

Mostly their victims surrendered without a fight. Pirate ships were full of dangerous fighting men, while most merchant ships had small crews of ordinary seamen. Once the captain of a merchant ship saw the pirate flag being hoisted, he knew he would almost certainly be killed in a fight. If he surrendered he would almost certainly survive.

What was a 'round robin'?

A round robin was the name for the list of the members of a pirate crew. No one wanted their name to be first on the list, because, if they were captured the authorities would think they had started the pirate group. So the crew signed their names in a circle – a round robin.

Where is Captain Kidd's treasure?

No one knows! Captain Kidd was a British ship owner who turned to piracy and made a huge fortune. When he was arrested and executed no one knew where his treasure had been hidden. A small amount was found on Gardiners Island off the east coast of the USA in 1699, but people have been searching for the rest of Kidd's treasure ever since.

Blackbeard and some members of his pirate army board a merchant ship.

What happened to people who fought with pirates?

Once the pirates realised you were planning to fight them, they would raise the red flag. This meant that there would be 'no quarter' – the loser would be shown no mercy and killed.

What was the punishment for piracy?

Almost all pirates who were captured were executed. The only exceptions were musicians and surgeons. There was such a shortage of both that they were almost always given the chance to join the navy instead of being put to death.

Were there ever any women pirates?

Mary Read and Anne Bonney were women pirates, but there were very few.

A pirate ship sails into the distance, with the Jolly Roger flag flying. This flag, showing a skull and crossbones, was designed to strike fear into the hearts of potential victims.

How did you get to be a pirate captain?

Pirate captains were elected by the crew. All the men on the ship met in what was called a 'foc'sle council' and debated who would be the best captain. A captain could also be removed by the foc'sle council.

How did you join a pirate crew?

Most pirates came from captured ships. Often the conditions on the ships they had come from were so bad that it seemed better to join the pirates than to go back to the old life.

Where did pirates go for their holidays?

One of the favourite places for pirates to go to spend their money was Port Royal in Jamaica. It was a lawless place, and when the city was destroyed by an earthquake some people said it was a judgement on the terrible things that had happened there. Another pirate holiday spot was New York in the America – during the 1690s many pirates from the Red Sea visited the city to relax.

MODERN PIRATES

There are still pirates around today. In the seas around the Caribbean, the same seas that Blackbeard sailed, modern-day pirates ambush the boats of wealthy people and steal their possessions. The seas of Southeast Asia also have regular incidents of piracy.

Why was Elizabeth I called 'The Virgin Queen'?

Because she never married, although she did have a number of men who wanted to marry her. Robert Dudley, one man she was thought likely to marry, was suspected of murdering his wife. Elizabeth rejected an offer of marriage from King Philip II of Spain, who later sent an army to invade England. And her first boyfriend, Thomas Seymour, was executed for trying to gain power over the throne.

What else was Elizabeth I famous for?

She was known as the cleanest woman in England. It was once reported with amazement that she had four baths a year. At a time when people sometimes wore the same underwear until it rotted, this was pretty unusual!

Queen Elizabeth surrounded by her faithful courtiers.

LOSING POWER

Elizabeth I was so terrified of losing her throne that she couldn't bear to hear about other monarchs who had lost power. In one play by William Shakespeare, King Richard II is forced off the throne. The scene in which this happened was never performed during Queen Elizabeth's reign!

Which queen saved England from invasion?

Elizabeth I, who ruled England from 1558 to 1603. She was one of Britain's most successful and popular monarchs, and managed to keep England safe from invasion throughout her reign.

Anyone accused of plotting against Elizabeth I risked death, as her cousin Mary Queen of Scots discovered. Mary had her head chopped off in 1587.

What was the Armada?

A fleet sent from Spain to invade England. It was meant to meet up with a Spanish army from the Netherlands and replace Elizabeth with a Catholic ruler. Elizabeth gave a famous speech to encourage her forces to fight the French, saying that though she was a 'weak and feeble woman' she had the heart of a man. The Armada was subsequently defeated.

Was Elizabeth I really a 'weak and feeble woman'?

No! Elizabeth used to beat up her courtiers and throw shoes at them if she was displeased. Her secretary, William Davison, quite often got punched and kicked when Elizabeth was upset.

Which other tough queens have there been?

One of the toughest must have been the warrior-queen from Roman times called Boudicca. One story about her says that she used to ride her chariot into battle without any clothes on.

Which queen lasted the longest?

Queen Victoria, who ruled from 1837 to 1901 – 64 years! Victoria was a popular queen, but she still had enemies. During her reign she survived seven assassination attempts. One of these was a repeat of an attempt to kill her the day before. The second time the police caught the gunman and discovered that his gun was loaded with blanks. He was still executed.

Which queen executed the most people?

Mary I, Elizabeth I's sister, executed as many people in her 5 years as queen as Elizabeth did in 45 years as monarch. Anyone who refused to convert to Catholicism, Mary's religion, risked being burned at the stake. Two hundred and eighty three people, including the Archbishop of Canterbury, were put to death in this way.

CHAMPION QUEEN

Queen Victoria was a great dog-lover – so much so that her pets won prizes at the Crufts dog show.

George IV drives his horses on in order to win a bet.

Which prince drove his coach recklessly to win a bet?

The Prince Regent, who later became George IV (the most unpopular English king ever!). He was famously fat, and his friends thought it would be impossible for horses to pull him up a steep hill. He leapt up and whipped the horses until they pulled the coach up the hill, winning the bet.

AND DON'T COME BACK!

George IV had a wife – his cousin, Caroline, but he hated her. George offered her £50,000 a year to stay out of the country once he became king. She refused and returned to England, but was locked out of the king's coronation ceremony!

Which dastardly king kept his wife a prisoner?

George I, who was also known as German George. He found out that his wife had a boyfriend and was so annoyed that he had the boyfriend strangled. He kept his wife locked in her room from that day onwards. Unknown to her, he had also stuffed the boyfriend's body under the floorboards.

Why was George I called German George?

Because he was from a German family, and never bothered to learn to speak English when he became king in 1714. Even though he ruled for 13 years until 1727, he only ever spoke German or French.

Was German George popular?

Yes and no. The ordinary people generally hated him, but Parliament loved him. Because he couldn't speak English he didn't understand much of what was going on. Parliament could get on with running the country without too much interference from the king.

Which queen had a rude rhyme made up about her?

Caroline, the wife of George II (German George's son), was so unpopular that children in the street chanted rhymes about her. 'Queen Queen Caroline, dipped her nose in turpentine, turpentine to make it shine, poor queen Caroline!'

Who was the last British king to lead his army into battle?

George II, but he didn't make a very good job of it. At the age of 60 he appeared in front of his troops at a battle with the French. Unfortunately his horse wasn't in a fighting mood – it turned round and started trotting back the way it had come. George couldn't control his horse and became a laughing stock.

Which king once adopted a pillow?

Throughout the reign of George III (from 1760 to1820) the king was plagued by mental illness, which led to some strange episodes. On one occasion he told his courtiers that he had adopted a new son called Octavius. When they came over to look at the child, they discovered that it was actually a pillow.

Which king died from overeating?

George IV again. He was so greedy that stories about his overeating became famous. Stories of him eating three or four chickens at a time made him very unpopular with his subjects, many of whom rarely had enough food. When George IV died in 1830 it was because of the strain on his heart caused by being so overweight.

What was George IV's biggest mistake?

One of the main reasons that people hated George was that he couldn't stop spending money – money he got from the taxpayers! His biggest mistake ever was to build a Royal Pavilion in Brighton, a seaside town near London. Originally a farmhouse, by the time the prince had finished with it the Pavilion looked like an Oriental palace. It cost a fortune and made him very unpopular.

George IV entertained his many friends at lavish parties in the newly-built Brighton Pavilion.

MURDEROUS WAYS

The body snatchers Burke and Hare perfected a way of killing their victims that left almost no trace that they had been murdered. They would get the person drunk on whisky, then Burke would lie across the body to keep it still, while Hare held a small pillow across the victim's mouth. The unlucky person would die of suffocation.

Who were the 'sack-em-up men'?

The 'sack-em-up men' were otherwise known as grave robbers or body snatchers. They used to dig up recently buried bodies and sell them.

Who would want to buy a dead body?

Doctors who wanted to do experiments. In the early 1800s doctors still didn't understand how the human body worked, and the only way to find out was to take one to pieces. Since you couldn't do this on a live person, you needed to get hold of a dead one.

Why did doctors have to buy stolen bodies?

The only bodies anyone was allowed to experiment on were the bodies of criminals who had been hanged. But there weren't enough of these to go round.

A doctor instructs grave robbers how to dig up a recently buried body.

Were there any other names for the body snatchers?

Yes, they were sometimes called 'resurrection men'. This was because they brought the dead back from the grave.

How much could you get for a dead body in the 1800s?

The going rate was about £3, which was a lot of money in those days. Fresher bodies fetched more: a really new one might get as much as £7.

Where can you see the skeleton of a snatched body?

In the Royal College of Surgeons in London. It is the body of Jonathon Wild, a master criminal whose body was bought by a doctor called William Cheselden. Cheselden liked to look inside criminals and see if they were different from law-abiding citizens.

William Burke.　　　William Hare.

Who were the most famous body snatchers?

William Burke and William Hare, who were actually murderers rather than body snatchers. Hare ran a guest house in Edinburgh, and Burke lived with him. When one of the guests died, they sold the body to a local doctor for £7. Then the two decided that they would start killing guests to sell the bodies, instead of waiting for them to die.

What happened to Burke and Hare?

One of the guests at Hare's guest house discovered a murdered body they had hidden and went to the police. The two men were questioned and claimed that the dead person had died of natural causes. But then in 1829 Hare told the police that it had been Burke who did the killing. Burke was hanged while Hare was allowed to live.

How many people did Burke and Hare kill?

Although the exact figure is not certain, it was between 13 and 30 people!

What happened to Burke's body after his execution?

Rather grotesquely, his skeleton was preserved and kept in Scotland and his skin was made into several objects, including a wallet!

Who was the most famous highwayman?

Dick Turpin, who terrorised the travellers of Essex and Yorkshire from 1735 to 1739. His cry 'Stand and deliver!' struck fear into travellers who knew they would have to give up their riches or be killed.

Was being a highwayman a good job?

There were some good things about it: you could earn a lot of money in a short space of time. But you might have to kill people who refused to give you their possessions – and if you got caught you would certainly be hanged.

What did Dick Turpin do before he was a highwayman?

Turpin first worked as a butcher, but was caught stealing cattle (which he was planning to sell in his shop). He then joined a gang of smugglers and deer poachers in Essex. They were called the Gregory Gang because three of the members came from the Gregory family. The gang was disbanded by the authorities and Dick needed to find some other way of making a living.

Dick Turpin prepares to hold up another carriage.

How did Dick Turpin become a highwayman?

He went into partnership with a man named Tom King, who was already a famous highwayman. Turpin accidentally shot and killed his partner while trying to shoot a policeman. From then on Turpin worked alone.

How many robberies did Dick Turpin commit?

No one knows for sure, because there were other highwaymen around at the time and it was hard to know who had committed particular robberies. But by the time Turpin was 30 years old there was a reward of £200 for his capture. He fled to Holland to escape the police.

How was Dick Turpin finally caught?

Having returned to England using a false name, Turpin was arrested in the town of Brough for shooting a cockerel. He was taken to court and then put in prison because he couldn't pay the fine. All the time the authorities still didn't know who he really was.

How was Dick Turpin's true identity discovered?

He wrote to his brother-in-law asking him to help pay the fine for killing the cockerel. Turpin's old schoolteacher saw the letter and recognised the writing. He travelled to York, where Dick was in prison, and identified him as Dick Turpin the highwayman. The teacher got the £200 reward and Dick Turpin was hanged.

What's the difference between a highwayman and a footpad?

Highwaymen rode a horse, which made it easier to catch carriages and then escape after the robbery. Footpads were on foot.

Many highwaymen ended up at the gallows.

How were highwaymen punished?

They were hanged by the neck. Then their bodies were put in gibbets, which were iron cages. The gibbets were hung in public places and the bodies displayed as a warning to others who were thinking of becoming highwaymen.

Who was Black Bess?

Most people think that Black Bess was the name of Dick Turpin's horse. In fact he never had a horse with this name. Black Bess was made up 97 years after Dick had been hanged, by a writer called Harrison Ainsworth in a book called *Rookwood*.

Who was 'Swift Nick'?

Swift Nick was the name King Charles II gave to a highwayman called John Nevison. Nevison once rode from London to York in a day – a journey of over 300 km. When he was arrested for a robbery he had committed in London one morning, Nevison produced the Lord Mayor of York as a witness that he had been in York in the evening. The jury didn't think it was possible to make the journey to London in a day, and Nevison was freed.

ESCAPE THROUGH THE SNOW!

Legend says that the highwayman John Nevison once escaped through a snowstorm by fitting his horse's shoes on backwards. The people trying to catch him thought he had gone in the opposite direction!

Sweeny Todd, ready to shave – and murder – his next customer!

What did Sweeny Todd do with his victims?

In the story, Sweeny Todd gave the bodies to the owner of the pie shop next door to his barbers. She made them into pies that were famous throughout London.

Who was the man they couldn't hang?

John Lee was sentenced to hang for the murder of his employer. The first time they tried to hang him, the trapdoor on the gallows broke. The second time, the trapdoor refused to work again. The trapdoor was tested and worked perfectly . . . until they tried to hang John Lee for a third time. The trapdoor failed again! In the end, the authorities decided that Lee's sentence should be changed to life imprisonment.

How were Victorian criminals punished?

Many were hanged, but other criminals were sent to prison where they were forced to do hard physical labour. Britain also used to send some of its criminals to Australia, a punishment called 'transportation'.

Who was Mary Anne Cotton?

Mary Anne Cotton was a far worse killer than the infamous Victorian murderer Jack the Ripper. She murdered between 15 and 20 people, some of whom were her husbands (she had at least three) and children. They all died of arsenic poisoning.

How did Mary Anne Cotton get away with killing so many people?

She moved from place to place and often changed her name.

Who was Sweeny Todd the Demon Barber?

Sweeny Todd was a fictional murderer. He lured people into his barber's shop, then just as they thought they were going to be shaved, their chair tipped backwards. They fell through a trapdoor and they broke their necks in the fall.

MARY ANNE COTTON

Victorian children made up a rhyme about Mary Anne Cotton that they would sing in the streets: 'Mary Anne Cotton. She's dead and she's rotten. She lies in her bed With her eyes wide open. Sing, sing, oh what can I sing? Mary Anne Cotton is tied up with string. Where? Where? Up in the air. Selling black puddings a penny a pair.'

Who was the most villainous Victorian?

The Victorian murderer Jack the Ripper was the most feared villain of Victorian times. He killed at least 5 women in London's Whitechapel district. The first was killed in August 1888 and the last died in November of the same year.

What was Jack the Ripper's real name?

No one knows as he was never caught. At the time of the murders the police got letters from someone who claimed to be the killer, which were signed 'Jack the Ripper'. The killer has been known by that name ever since.

Who did people think the Ripper might be?

There were lots of theories about who the Ripper really was. One of the most popular was that he was the Duke of Clarence, Queen Victoria's oldest grandson.

Jack the Ripper hits the headlines.

What was the 'Crime of the Century'?

An event also called the Great Train Robbery took place on August 8, 1963. A gang of 15 men wearing ski masks and crash helmets stopped a mail train heading from Glasgow to London and stole the contents. They were led by a man named Bruce Reynolds.

What was the train carrying?

Used bank notes that were being taken to London to be destroyed. The men stole 120 mail bags which altogether contained about £2.6 million.

How did the robbers know the money was on the train?

They had inside information given to them by someone who worked for the Royal Mail. To this day no one knows who this person was.

How did the robbers stop the train?

They used a battery to change a signal from green to red. The train's fireman went to investigate and was captured by the gang. Then the driver was forced to move the train beside a road, where the gang loaded their booty into cars and fled.

Was anyone hurt in the robbery?

The train driver, whose name was Jack Mills, was hit on the head with a cosh by one of the gang, Buster Edwards. Mills never fully recovered and died a few years later.

The train robbers unload the sacks of used notes into their jeeps.

Who was the most famous Great Train robber?

Ronnie Biggs, who escaped from prison in 1965 with another robber, Charlie Wilson. Biggs had plastic surgery to disguise himself, and fled to Paris then Australia, before finally settling down in Brazil. In May 2001, he returned to England and was arrested.

How long did the robbers go to prison for?

Twelve of the 15 robbers were caught and sent to prison for a total of 307 years. None of them ended up serving more than 13 years.

Ronnie Biggs.

How were the Great Train robbers caught?

After the robbery they hid out at Leatherslade Farm in Buckinghamshire. Once the robbers had divided up the money and left, another gang was hired to burn down the farmhouse to destroy any evidence. They did such a bad job that the police found everyone's fingerprints.

THE GREAT TRAIN ROBBERY MOVIE

The robbery that took place in 1963 got its name from a film made in 1903. The film was a very early moving picture, one of the first in which the camera, as well as the actors, moved around. Its plot was inspired by the hold-ups of the Wild West.

How did Sherlock Holmes help win the First World War?

Doyle wrote several short stories that showed Holmes outwitting German spies. The stories were meant to encourage people to think that Britain would win the war.

Who was Professor Moriarty?

Sherlock Holmes' greatest enemy, a criminal genius who also lived in London. Moriarty controlled most of the criminal activity in the city, and always managed to escape Holmes at the last moment. Holmes finally caught up with him after chasing the master criminal across Europe. Moriarty was killed falling from the Reichenbach Falls in Switzerland.

Holmes and Watson – Holmes' friend and helper – watch as the Hound of the Baskervilles attacks a victim.

Who invented Sherlock Holmes?

A writer named Arthur Conan Doyle. Doyle's first Sherlock Holmes story was published in 1887. In the end he wrote four novels and 56 short stories about Holmes. When Doyle got bored with writing about Holmes he wrote that the detective had died while struggling with the master criminal Professor Moriarty. There were so many protests that Doyle was forced to bring Holmes back to life again and continue writing about him.

What was the Hound of the Baskervilles?

The Hound of the Baskervilles was a giant creature that featured in one of the cases of the fictional detective Sherlock Holmes. It was a demon hound that haunted the Baskerville family. Holmes was called in when one of the Baskervilles was apparently killed by the Hound.

LEGEND OF THE HOUND

In the story *Hound of the Baskervilles*, legend said that the Hound first appeared in ancient times, when a particularly evil member of the family sold himself to the Devil in order to get his own way. Ever since, the demonic Hound has haunted his heirs.

What kind of villains were the Krays?

The Krays were said to be involved in murders, violence, protection rackets, gang wars, gambling and robberies. They were identical twins, born in the East End of London in 1933. The brothers had a stylish image and became famous in London for their sharp dressing as much as their criminal activities.

Who were the Kray twins?

They ran a criminal gang in the East End of London. The Krays were in charge of most crime that was committed in the area, and were famous for their brutality. They were suspected of several murders, and in the end they were convicted of killing a man called Jack 'The Hat' Macvitie.

Were the Krays heroes or villains?

To some people in the East End of London they seemed like heroes. The Krays made sure that the only crime being committed was by them, so minor crimes like burglary were less common when the Krays were in charge. But the twins were really villains: they were only in charge because they hurt or killed people who got in their way.

Who was Nipper of the Yard?

One of the most famous real-life detectives in Britain was a detective from Scotland Yard called Read whose nickname was 'Nipper'. He caught the notorious criminals, the Kray twins.

Nipper of the Yard is interviewed about the investigation of the Kray twins.

Which heroine rowed her way to fame?

Grace Darling, who was the daughter of the keeper of the Longstone Lighthouse in Bamburgh, on the coast of Northumberland. When she was just 23 years old she became a national hero in Britain for taking part in a dramatic rescue.

Who did Grace Darling rescue?

On the night of September 6, 1838 there was a great storm off the coast. A ship named the *Forfarshire* ran aground on the Farne islands, near Grace's father's lighthouse. In the morning a small group of survivors was spotted clinging to some rocks: Grace and her father set out in a small open boat to rescue them.

How did Grace become a tourist attraction?

Pleasure boat trips were organised to take people to the Longstone Lighthouse for a glimpse of her.

What happened to Grace?

Sadly she was not as strong as people thought. Within a short time Grace had contracted flu and then pneumonia. She died in October 1842, four years after her heroic rescue.

How did Grace Darling become a national heroine?

The national newspapers got to hear about the rescue and Grace rapidly became famous. Newspaper and magazine articles and poems were written about her, and many paintings were made of the rescue and of Grace.

Grace rows out to rescue the crew of the stricken ship, Forfarshire.

Who were the suffragettes?

Women demonstrators demand the right to vote.

They were a group of women led by Emmeline Pankhurst, who in 1903 began to campaign for women to be allowed to vote in elections. (At that time only men were allowed to vote.) The suffragettes went on marches, shouted at politicians in public meetings, and even took their own lives as a form of protest. Women won the right to vote in 1928.

Why were they called suffragettes?

Because the right to vote is called suffrage. The women wanted universal suffrage – the right for everyone to vote – so they became known as suffragettes. The official name of the group was the Women's Social and Political Union.

PRESS GANGS

Life was extremely hard for a sailor in the Royal Navy in Nelson's time. In fact, it was so hard that the navy found it almost impossible to get anyone to join. Instead they sent 'press gangs' into seaside towns to kidnap men to serve on the ships. Once the ships had left, it could be years before the men got home again, if they ever did.

Who was Britain's greatest sailor?

Britain's greatest wartime sea captain was Admiral Horatio Nelson. Nelson won famous victories at the time of the Napoleonic wars. At the Battle of the Nile he pretended not to see an order to withdraw from the fight and went on to win. But his most famous victory was at the Battle of Trafalgar in 1805, where he defeated the French fleet and prevented an invasion of Britain.

How did Nelson manage to miss an order to retreat?

He was blind in one eye because of an injury from an earlier battle, so he held his telescope up to his blind eye and said he couldn't see the order to leave the battle.

Where is Nelson's ship today?

Nelson's flagship, called HMS *Victory*, is in a dry dock in Portsmouth, England. Thousands of people visit it each year.

What was life like in Nelson's navy?

Life was very hard, especially for ordinary sailors. They slept in hammocks that almost touched the hammock next door, ate terrible food and were subject to very harsh discipline. Even the officers did little better – the only person to have his own cabin on most ships was the captain.

Nelson watches the battle through his telescope.

Who played bowls while a Spanish invasion fleet arrived?

Sir Francis Drake was playing a game of bowls in Plymouth, in 1588, when news reached him that the Spanish Armada had been sighted. He calmly finished his game before heading off to do battle. The Armada was later defeated by a combination of the British navy and a terrible storm that wrecked many Spanish ships.

Which sea captain was the first Briton to sail round the world?

Sir Francis Drake, who sailed his ship, *Golden Hind*, across the Atlantic, round the southern tip of South America, through the Pacific and back into the Atlantic past the southern tip of Africa. The feat had only been managed once before, by a Spanish expedition led by Ferdinand Magellan.

Who was the greatest British voyager?

Captain James Cook, who was born in 1728, journeyed all round the world. He made two visits in search of *terra australis incognita*, which is Latin for 'unknown southern land' – what we now call Antarctica. He also visited Australia, New Zealand, Easter Island, Tonga and the Hawaiian islands.

How did Captain Cook die?

By the time Cook revisited Hawaii in 1779, the islanders were starting to realise that he might not be a god. When they gathered around him on the beach he was unable to escape by swimming out to his boat. Seeing that he was obviously not a god, the islanders killed Cook.

Captain Cook meets his end in Hawaii.

Who thought Captain Cook was a god?

The Hawaiian islanders thought Cook was the god Lono, since an ancient legend told that Lono would one day return to the islands bearing a banner similar to the white sails of Cook's ship.

SURFING IN HAWAII

Cook and his crew were among the first white people to see the sport of surfing. Lieutenant James King, who continued Cook's record of their voyage after he died, wrote of Hawaiians being 'driven along with amazing rapidity toward the shore' on their surfboards. Lieutenant King wrote that their 'boldness ... was scarcely to be credited'.

Captain Oates struggles out into the horrific Antarctic conditions.

Who stepped out for a short while?

Captain Oates, a member of Scott's expedition. Knowing that he was too weak to finish the journey, he left the expedition's tent with the words 'I may be some time'. Oates had decided to die in the hope that the expedition would move faster without him and that some of them would survive.

Who lost the race to the South Pole?

Captain Scott – often called Scott of the Antarctic. He became a national hero in Britain in 1912, even though his attempt to be the first person to reach the South Pole failed.

What disaster beset the party?

Just as they were nearing the Pole one of the party slipped and injured himself. From then on he had to be carried on the sledge. This slowed the party down a lot.

How far was Scott from safety when he died?

Scott and his men died just 18 km from the supplies that could have saved their lives.

Why did Scott lose the race to the South Pole?

He was beaten by the Norwegian explorer Roald Amundsen. Amundsen used a shorter route and dog sleds, while Scott went a longer way and dragged his supplies along himself.

When did Amundsen reach the Pole?

He arrived there on December 14, 1911. Scott arrived almost a month later, on January 18, 1912. When Scott arrived he found a note from Amundsen saying how sorry he was that one of them had to lose the race.

Who first climbed Mount Everest?

Two men called Edmund Hillary and Sherpa Tensing Norkey, members of a British expedition, reached the summit of Everest on May 29, 1953.

Who was George Mallory?

Mallory was one of a pair of climbers (the other was named Andrew Irvine) who tried to climb Everest in June 1924. They were last spotted moving towards the Second Step, a climb just below the summit. The climber who saw them, Noel Odell, later said that 'I think myself that there is a strong probability that Mallory and Irvine succeeded'. But we'll never know for certain because both climbers died on the mountain.

What equipment did early climbers use on Everest?

The very earliest climbers had almost no special equipment at all. George Mallory, for example, was wearing a wool suit, a button-down shirt and wool long johns. He and Irvine carried ice axes to help them grip, and took bottled oxygen to help them breathe, but the tanks of oxygen weighed 15 kg!

Who was Tensing Norkey?

Often called Sherpa Tensing, he was an experienced guide from Nepal. Tensing had worked for European expeditions since 1935, and was the most experienced Himalayan climber on the 1953 expedition.

SHERPAS

The Sherpas are people who live in north-eastern Nepal, in the very highest valleys. They often take part in climbing expeditions, because they are used to working in the thin air of the highest mountains.

Which explorer lost his ship to the ice?

Ernest Shackleton took 28 men on an expedition to the South Pole. He never made it to the Pole because his ship became trapped in the ice. Despite the most horrendous weather conditions, Shackleton managed to rescue all of his men.

Shackleton's ship sits motionless, trapped in the ice off Antarctica.

Who rode on Chariots of Fire?

The sprinter Harold Abrahams, who won the 100 metres sprint race at the 1924 Paris Olympics. Abrahams was Jewish, and at that time it was difficult for Jewish people to be socially accepted in Britain. He overcame many obstacles to win the race and became a national hero. The story of Abrahams and his team-mates was made into an Oscar-winning film called *Chariots of Fire* in 1981.

Who broke the four-minute mile?

A British runner called Roger Bannister. On May 6, 1954, in a small race in Oxford, Bannister ran a mile in 3 minutes 59.4 seconds. He was the first person in the world ever to break the four-minute barrier for a mile-long run.

Harold Abrahams surges through the finish line, winning a gold medal for Britain.

MOTOR RACING WORLD CHAMPIONS

The Formula One World Championship has been won by British drivers 12 times since 1950:

1958	Mike Hawthorne	1969	Jackie Stewart
1962	Graham Hill	1971	Jackie Stewart
1963	Jim Clark	1973	Jackie Stewart
1964	John Surtees	1976	James Hunt
1965	Jim Clark	1992	Nigel Mansell
1968	Graham Hill	1996	Damon Hill

Which other Britons have won Abrahams' sprint title?

Alan Wells won the 100 m sprint at the 1980 Olympics and Linford Christie won the 100 m at the Barcelona Games in 1992.

Which British woman won the heptathlon in 2000?

Denise Lewis, who won the gold medal even though she had an injury during the competition.

Which British racing driver was both Formula One champion and Indy Car champion?

Nigel Mansell, who won the Formula One championship in 1992 with the Williams-Renault team. He then went to North America to race in the Indy Car championship. In 1993, his first year in Indy Car racing, Mansell drove his Newman-Hass car to victory. The team was part-owned by the famous American actor Paul Newman.

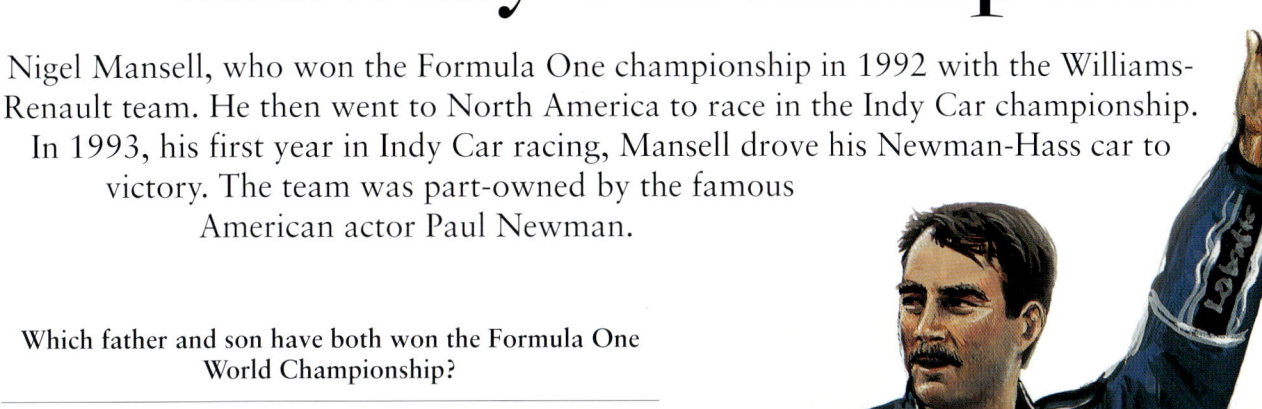

Which father and son have both won the Formula One World Championship?

Graham Hill, one of the most brilliant drivers of his day, won the world championship in 1962 and 1968. He was tragically killed in a plane crash not long after, but his son Damon grew up to win the title in 1996.

Who is Britain's greatest-ever Olympic competitor?

Steve Redgrave, the rower who has won gold medals at five consecutive games: Sydney in 2000; Atlanta in 1996; Barcelona in 1992; Seoul in 1988; and Los Angeles in 1984.

What was the most unusual Olympic event?

Probably one of the shooting events at the 1912 London Olympics. Today competitors shoot at clay pigeons – small discs made of clay that are thrown into the air by a machine. But in London in 1912 they shot at real pigeons, which were released from a cage.

Nigel Mansell won 31 Grand Prix out of the 185 that he competed in – a brilliant record.

Disaster and Disease

Which disasters are caused by the weather?

Wherever people live on our planet, the local weather can cause disasters. In the Caribbean, there are hurricanes. In North Africa, the greatest danger comes from drought. Britain is surrounded by sea, criss-crossed with rivers and has heavy rainfall, and the commonest disaster caused by the weather is flooding.

Why is flooding worst in the south and east of Britain?

The south and east are the flattest, lowest-lying parts of Britain. Our island is also gradually tilting over to one side. The north and west of Scotland are slowly rising out of the sea, while the south and east are sinking at the rate of about 30 cm every hundred years. The East Anglian coast is falling into the sea at the rate of about 1m a year.

The citizens of Dunwich in East Anglia wade through floodwaters hoping to save their belongings.

How did the Moon cause floods in eastern England?

It is the gravitational pull of the moon which causes the sea to rise in tides. Twice each month the moon and the sun line up so that they both pull on the sea at the same time. This causes the highest tides, called 'spring' tides, and the worst flooding. In March 1947 high tides combined with a stormy sea and rivers which were swollen by melting snow. Most of eastern England, from Yorkshire to Essex, was flooded.

Which port was lost to the sea?

In 1200, the most important East Anglian port was a place called Dunwich. From the 13th to the 18th centuries, the town was washed little by little into the sea in a series of disastrous floods. One of the worst floods occurred in the thirteenth century and it destroyed 400 houses. In the sixteenth century, four churches disappeared beneath the waves.

Stranded householders wait for their rescuers in Canvey Island.

What was the first known flood in British history?

Ten thousand years ago Britain was joined onto Europe, and the first people to live here arrived on foot. They were able to do this because sea levels were much lower and much of the water was frozen and locked up in ice caps. Between 8000 BC and 6500 BC the weather warmed up, melting the ice and causing massive flooding. Some 260,000 square kilometres of Britain was covered by the North Sea, while a new channel cut Britain off from Europe.

What was the 'lost land' of Lyonesse?

Around Britain many stories are told of lands lost to the sea. In Cornwall people tell stories of a rich kingdom, called Lyonesse, which was destroyed by a flood. They say that only the mountain peaks of Lyonesse can still be seen, and that these are the Isles of Scilly.

Why do rivers flood in March?

After a snowy winter, the weather warms in March, causing snow and ice to melt. This can happen rapidly and, if there is also heavy rainfall, rivers can rise and burst their banks. This happened to the River Thames in March 1744, causing the worst flooding of the 1700s.

STORMY WEATHER

Throughout late January 1953 there were violent storms in the North Sea. On the last night of the month the waves, which were now almost 9 m high, broke through the sea wall which protected Canvey Island in Essex. This low-lying island was soon covered with water, and the inhabitants had to climb onto their roofs to wait for help. This was the worst flood of the twentieth century. It caused the deaths of 307 people – 58 of them on Canvey Island.

When was Britain's worst storm?

The worst storm on record struck southern England on the night of Friday November 26, 1703. It caused winds that reached speeds of 190 km/h. The storm destroyed 800 houses and ripped the roofs off many more. Fifteen ships sank, drowning more than 1,000 sailors. It is thought that around 8,000 people were killed in total.

What causes terrible storms to hit Britain?

Storms often begin across the Atlantic Ocean as hurricanes, which then make their way eastwards and strike Britain. Usually they lose their power as they go, but on rare occasions they strike Britain with all their force.

Where does the name hurricane come from?

The word 'hurricane' comes from *huracan*, the name given by the ancient Taino people of the Caribbean to their god of the wild wind. It was probably a Caribbean hurricane that hit Britain in 1703.

MODERN STORM

In October 1987 a hurricane struck southern England, tearing up 15,000,000 trees and blocking roads and railways. Although the storm was severe it only killed 18 people because it struck at night, when most people were in bed. If the storm had hit the country in the daytime when the roads were busy, many more would have died.

Which place suffered the worst damage during the 1703 storm?

The worst storm damage occurred in the port of Bristol. A surge of water rushed up the River Severn, flooding the city and the surrounding fields. It is thought that 15,000 sheep drowned.

How do we know so much about the storm of 1703?

This storm was so unusual that a writer called Daniel Defoe decided to write a book about it. He travelled around the country collecting people's stories about the incredible storm and published them in his book – *The Storm*.

What is a tornado?

A tornado is a whirling column of wind which can move across land or sea, uprooting trees and tearing roofs off houses or causing waterspouts. On May 21, 1950 a group of three tornadoes travelled 110 km from Buckinghamshire to Cambridgeshire, creating huge amounts of damage.

What happened to the model of the Eddystone lighthouse?

In his book, *The Storm*, Daniel Defoe wrote, 'It is remarkable that at the same time the lighthouse was blown down, the model of it, in Mr Winstanley's home at Littlebury in Essex, above 200 miles from the lighthouse, fell down and broke to pieces.'

What was the Eddystone lighthouse?

In 1698, a London merchant called Henry Winstanley designed and built a wooden lighthouse on the Eddystone rocks in the sea south of Plymouth. After a year, realising that it was not strong enough to withstand the weather, he rebuilt it with stronger walls. Winstanley was now so confident about his lighthouse that he said that he would feel safe there, even during 'the greatest storm that ever was'. In November 1703, after two weeks of heavy gales, the wind dropped and Winstanley rowed out to the lighthouse to see how it was coping.

What happened to the Eddystone lighthouse and its designer?

The great storm struck the lighthouse at midnight on a Friday – the very day that Winstanley had chosen to visit his lighthouse. The following Saturday morning, the lighthouse, along with its designer, had vanished.

The supposedly indestructible lighthouse at Eddystone is smashed to pieces by the storms of 1703.

Why did cathedrals collapse?

The biggest buildings of the Middle Ages were the great churches, called cathedrals. Each city wanted to have a taller and grander cathedral than the others. As a result, the builders often overreached themselves, building walls and spires which were too high, on foundations (bases) which were not solid and with roofs which were not properly supported.

Why shouldn't you build on marshy ground?

Choosing a marshy spot to build on was one reason why cathedrals tended to fall down. The cathedrals at Ely, Winchester and Carlisle were all built on marshy ground, where the weight of the buildings made them sink and tilt to one side. The result was that the towers of all three cathedrals fell down: Winchester in 1107, Ely in 1322 and Carlisle in 1380.

Which cathedrals were damaged by earthquakes?

An earthquake is caused by movements in the plates that make up the earth's surface. During an earthquake the ground beneath our feet shakes and buildings rock. Earthquakes caused the roofs to collapse at Lincoln cathedral in 1185, and at Wells cathedral in 1248.

How did the Victorians build such enormous buildings?

After the cathedrals of the Middle Ages, the biggest buildings were put up in the Victorian age (1837-1901). This was thanks to a new building material: cast iron. With it the Victorians were able to build huge buildings with enormous roofs, such as railway stations and long railway bridges that spanned wide rivers.

The spire at Lincoln cathedral collapses after being hit by a gale.

Which cathedral has suffered the most disasters?

Lincoln Cathedral has had the worst luck. In 1141 fire destroyed the wooden roof. This was replaced by a stone roof, which fell down in 1185. The next disaster was in the thirteenth century, when the central tower collapsed. Then in the sixteenth century, the wooden spire was blown down in a gale.

Why do buildings fall down?

Ever since the Middle Ages big buildings have been known to topple over without warning. They are often brought down by gales, but a more common cause of such a disaster is simply that the building was badly constructed in the first place.

BRITISH EARTHQUAKES

There are around 200 earthquakes a year in Britain, though most are not strong enough to cause much damage. London suffered damage from earthquakes in 1382, 1580 and 1750. Only 11 people are ever known to have died as a result of British earthquakes.

A train plunges into the River Tay as the railway bridge beneath it collapses.

What was the worst Victorian building disaster?

In 1878 Thomas Bouch was proud to have finished overseeing the building of his 3 km-long railway bridge over the River Tay in Scotland. At the time this was the longest bridge in the world. The following year, on a stormy evening – December 28, 1879 – the central section of the bridge collapsed, taking with it the train and 75 passengers, who all died in the icy waters below.

Why did the Tay bridge collapse?

A strong gale was blowing at right angles to the bridge, and the bridge was not strong enough to take the force of the wind plus the weight of the train rushing over it.

Mary Rose sinks slowly into the sea.

Which warship sank under odd circumstances?

In 1545, a warship called the *Mary Rose* sank in the sea off Portsmouth. She had already sailed on many successful voyages, and the weather was not even rough at the time of the disaster. The reason why the *Mary Rose* sank remained a mystery until 1982, when the ship was raised from the seabed.

Why did *Mary Rose* sink?

This warship was the pride of King Henry VIII's fleet. Archaeologists learned that the *Mary Rose* had been refitted with bigger cannons, which made her top-heavy. When a sudden gust of wind caught the ship's sails, the extra weight made it roll to one side. Water poured in through the open gun ports, and the *Mary Rose* sank as King Henry watched from the shore.

Why are dozens of Spanish ships wrecked around Britain?

They are wrecks from the Armada, a 130-strong invasion fleet, sent by King Philip of Spain in 1588. The fleet was defeated in battle and then scattered by storms. The Armada tried to make its way home by sailing around the north of Scotland, where more of the ships sank in storms.

Which disaster led to a £20,000 prize being offered?

On October 22, 1707, a fleet of four English ships was wrecked off the Isles of Scilly, south-west of the UK, causing the death of admiral Sir Cloudsley Shovell and nearly 2,000 men. The disaster happened because the admiral had misjudged his longitude (position to the east or west). Sailors could easily find their latitude (position to the north or south) from the sun and stars, but they had no way of measuring how far east or west they had travelled. The government offered a huge prize – £20,000 – to anyone who could solve the problem.

Who won the prize?

The prize was won in 1773 by John Harrison, who invented the first clock which could keep accurate time at sea. By comparing local time, worked out by the sun's height, with the time back home, shown on Harrison's clock, a sailor could find out how far east or west he had travelled.

Why do ships sink?

The seas around the British Isles are littered with the wrecks of thousands of ships which date from all periods of our history. They range from ancient hollowed-out tree trunks, to sixteenth-century galleons, and modern oil tankers. They sank for many reasons. Some were driven onto rocks by strong winds or overwhelmed by high seas. Many were sunk in battle, while others simply lost their way in the dark and ran onto rocks.

'UNSINKABLE' SHIP?

In 1912 the British ocean liner *Titanic* was the biggest and most luxurious ship ever built. On April 15, during her first voyage, she hit an iceberg and sank. With her steel hull, the *Titanic* was believed to be unsinkable, so there were not enough lifeboats to carry all the passengers. Out of 2,300 people on board only about 700 were saved.

The last moments of the *Titanic*.

How can the cold kill?

Just like droughts and heavy rainfall, cold weather often led to famine. The winter of 1204–5 was so cold that the earth froze until March 25, stopping farmers from ploughing their fields and planting grain, as well as destroying the crops which had already been planted. Thousands of people starved to death.

What was the 'Little Ice Age'?

Between 1340 and 1850, the weather was much colder than it is today. There was a heavy snowfall every winter, and rivers and ponds often froze. In the winter of 1607–8, even the sea froze around some ports. The winter of 1606–7 was called the 'Great Winter', while the whole period from 1340–1850 is now known as the 'Little Ice Age'.

What was 'the year without a summer'?

In April 1815, a huge volcano exploded at Tambora, on the island of Sumbawa in Indonesia, sending up masses of dust into the upper atmosphere. The dust slowly circled the earth, causing beautiful red sunsets but also blocking out almost a third of the sun's heat. As a result, the summer of 1816 was so cold in Britain that there were snow drifts in July and severe frosts in September. Around the world, people remembered 1816 as 'the year without a summer'.

What was a frost fair?

Between 1629 and 1814, the River Thames at London froze over 23 times. Frost fairs were held on the ice, with stalls selling food and offering entertainments, such as puppet shows. People skated, danced, played football and staged horse races, and whole oxen were roasted above fires on the ice. The longest period of the great freeze was two months, in the winter of 1683–84, when the ice was said to be 28 cm thick. People called this the 'Great Frost'.

A frost fair on the River Thames.

A farmer searches for his flock of sheep that have become stranded in the snow.

When was the worst blizzard of the 1800s?

A blizzard is a severe snowstorm, with gale-force winds that push drifts of snow across the land. One of the worst blizzards took place from March 9–13 in 1891. Fierce easterly winds carried sheets of snow across southern England and Wales. In parts of London the snow was 3.5 m deep. Fourteen trains were buried under snow in Devon and 220 people were killed, most of them on the 65 ships that sank during the storm.

Why were thousands of sheep buried?

The 1891 blizzard arrived so suddenly that the shepherds had no time to round up their flocks of sheep, which were quickly buried in the deep snow. Several days later, the shepherds went out to look for the animals, prodding the snow with long sticks. Although 6,000 sheep and lambs died, amazingly, thousands more were brought out alive. They had survived thanks to their thick woolly coats.

Why did the Thames stop freezing?

One reason the Thames froze was that its currents were slowed down by the narrow spans of the old London Bridge: slow-moving water freezes easily. London Bridge was pulled down in 1831, and despite many bitterly cold winters since, the Thames has never frozen again.

When was leprosy common in Britain?

Leprosy may have been brought to Britain by the Romans in the first century AD. It remained here until the disease began to die out, for unknown reasons, in the late 1500s. However, it is likely that people suffering from all sorts of skin diseases were mistakenly described as lepers and that many people called lepers were probably not really lepers at all.

What is leprosy?

Leprosy is a disease which attacks the skin and nerves, turning the skin scaly, lumpy and blotchy. It can also cause the loss of fingers and toes. It is caused by a 'mycobacterium', a germ which looks like a tiny fungus under the microscope. Leprosy is very hard to catch – 95 per cent of people who come into contact with the germ don't catch the disease.

Why did lepers carry bells, clappers and poles?

In the Middle Ages, most people looked on leprosy with horror, and avoided the lepers' touch. So sufferers had to carry a clapper or bell to warn other people that they were approaching. They also carried a long pole to point at goods they wished to buy in the markets.

A leper carrying a bell and pole.

LAZARUS

In the Bible, Jesus Christ tells the story of a poor beggar, called Lazarus, who is covered with sores and who begs for crumbs at the gates of a rich man. When they both die, the rich man goes to hell, while Lazarus is carried by angels to heaven. This poor beggar might have been a leper.

What happened to people who caught leprosy?

They went to church where a special ceremony was carried out. The priest threw earth on their feet, saying 'Be thou dead to the world, but alive again to God'. They were then handed their staff and bell or clapper, and told the new rules by which they had to live. They could never enter a church again, or any crowded place, and they had to wear special clothing so that they could be identified.

Lepers, with a priest, at the ceremony which officially cast them out of normal society.

Where did lepers live?

If they were lucky, lepers lived in special houses called 'leprosaria', run by the Church or by town councils. Rich people often left money to care for lepers in their wills.

What was a leper squint?

In the east end of some medieval churches, you can still find a tiny window in the outside wall. Although lepers were not allowed to go inside the church, they could watch the services through this window, called the 'leper squint'.

What was a healing shrine?

Since Roman times, sick people have looked to religion for cures. They visited special holy places, called healing shrines, where they made vows (promises) and offerings to gods or saints who were believed to have healing powers.

What were the strangest medical treatments in Britain?

Throughout history, sick people have turned to all sorts of strange medical treatments in the hope of being cured of their ailments. These have included visiting the shrine of a god or saint, being touched by a king or queen and wearing magic charms.

What was a votive?

The Romans invented the practice of leaving a votive, a small model of the diseased part of the body, at the shrine. This was carried on by Christians in the Middle Ages, and continues to this day in Catholic and Greek Orthodox churches.

How did places become healing shrines?

Roman healing shrines were often linked with water, such as the hot spring at Bath, where a goddess called Sulis Minerva was worshipped. The Christian shrines of the Middle Ages were the tombs of saints.

Why did kings and queens touch sick people?

From the eleventh century until the early 1700s, kings and queens were believed to have the power to cure by touch. People suffering from a disease of the neck, called scrofula, or the 'king's evil', would visit the court to be touched. The practice reached a peak under King Charles II (1660–85) who touched 92,000 sufferers.

Sick pilgrims visit a healing shrine in a cathedral.

A 'toady' entertains the crowd in a local marketplace.

Could anyone else cure by touch?

From the sixteenth century, people believed that a seventh son had the power to heal by touch. In 1637 a five-year-old boy called Richard Gilbert, who was the seventh son of a Somerset farmer, held regular healing sessions in his home. He touched people's swellings, saying, 'I touch. God heals'.

What was a folk cure?

Folk cures were treatments made up by ordinary people. Until the eighteenth century, every village had 'cunning men' or 'wise women' who treated the sick with home-made medicines and charms. One cure, for toothache, was to write three times on a piece of paper 'Jesus Christ for mercy sake, Take away this toothache'. The paper was then burned.

Did toadys really eat toads?

Toads are highly poisonous. Some people think that the toady must have pretended to swallow the animal, using a trick to make it vanish. However, some scientists think that it would be possible to swallow a toad if it was first made used to being handled. Toads only give off poison when they are scared.

Why did people swallow live toads?

In the 1600s and 1700s, a common sight at fairs was a 'toady', a man who swallowed poisonous live toads for a living. The toad-eater was employed by a 'quack', or fake doctor. After swallowing the toad the man would fall to the ground in a faint. The quack would then bring him back to life with a potion, which he would then sell to the crowd as a 'cure-all' medicine.

MIND OVER MATTER

Modern science has shown that if you believe that a cure will work, it often will. So even a quack doctor's potion might have helped the Britons of the 1600s and 1700s get better if they believed in it.

Who has tried to destroy London?

The city of London was founded by the Romans in around AD 50. In the 2,000 years since then, the city has been the site of many disasters, including floods, outbreaks of plague and dozens of 'great fires'. Perhaps the worst disasters of all were those of wartime, when the city came under attack by enemies, including the Iceni in AD 60, the Vikings in 851, and the Germans in 1940.

What signs of Boudicca's attack can still be seen?

In more than a dozen places in London, archaeologists have uncovered a layer of red earth, around 45 cm thick, 4 m below the modern streets. This is all that remains of the wooden buildings of the Roman town that was burned by Boudicca.

Boudicca spurs her army on against the Romans.

What was the first London disaster?

Just ten years after London was founded on the Thames as a trading settlement, an East Anglian tribe called the Iceni rebelled against Roman rule. Led by their warrior queen, Boudicca, they sacked and burned Camulodonum (Colchester), London and Verulamium (St Albans). According to a Roman writer, Tacitus, the Iceni killed 70,000 people, taking no prisoners. The Roman army, which was away in the west at the time of the revolt, eventually defeated Boudicca in battle, and she killed herself.

Who attacked London from the air?

Who attacked London from the sea?

In the year 851, a fleet of 350 warships sailed up the River Thames and attacked London. They carried Vikings – warriors who had sailed across the sea from Scandinavia. The Vikings sacked London, killing many English people and taking others away as slaves. The Vikings returned to London in 872, this time to stay. They captured the city, which remained a Viking base for the next 14 years, until they were finally driven out by the English king, Alfred the Great.

What was the German air attack of London called?

The first air raid on London was just the beginning of a bombing campaign called the Blitz. Every night, from September 7 to November 13, London was attacked by around 160 German bombers. In total, around 6,000 people were killed.

On the late afternoon of September 7, 1940, 600 German bomber planes appeared in the sky over London. They dropped hundreds of fire bombs, which set the docks ablaze. Throughout the night, German bombers returned in waves, guided to the docks by the red glow of the fires. In one night, 430 Londoners were killed and 1,600 were injured.

What was the 'Great Fire Raid'?

On December 29, 1940, the German bombers attacked London again, and 150 planes dropped 600 fire bombs on the city. The fires the bombs caused spread, helped along by a strong westerly wind. Within two hours of the bombing raid, there were 1,500 fires burning. The river was at low tide, and the firemen were unable to find enough water to fight the flames.

The city of London burns as the fire bombs dropped by the German Air Force start fires across the capital.

THE BLITZ

The Blitz was just one campaign in the Second World War, which had started in September 1939. By the summer of 1940, the Germans had conquered Poland, France and Belgium. Only Britain remained fighting Germany, and the German leader, Adolf Hitler, wanted to force the British to make peace. He thought that the way to do this was to bomb British cities.

Victims of the plague are carried to mass graves.

What were the symptoms of the Black Death?

The symptoms could appear up to a week after being bitten by a flea from a black rat. The victims would suffer from headaches, aching limbs, a rash, vomiting and a high fever. Glands in their armpits, neck and groin would swell painfully. These swellings were called 'buboes', giving the disease its commonest name 'bubonic plague'. Three-quarters of sufferers would die within a week of developing symptoms.

What were pneumonic and septicemic plague?

The germ also caused two other forms of disease: pneumonic and septicemic plague. Pneumonic plague attacked the lungs and was spread by coughing. Septicemic plague attacked the blood and made the skin break out in dark blotches, which is where the name 'Black Death' came from. These forms were more deadly than bubonic plague, but less common because sufferers died too quickly to spread the disease.

Why did plague eventually disappear?

By the early 1700s, the bubonic plague had disappeared from most of Europe. It may be that the black rat which carried the disease was dying out. Perhaps it had been killed off by the plague. However, nobody knows why the plague disappeared, or whether it will ever come back again!

What was the Black Death?

The 'Black Death' was a name given to plague, a terrible disease which first appeared in eastern Asia in 1320. It then spread west, and reached England in 1348. By 1351, it had killed almost a third of the population of Britain.

PLAGUE DEATHS IN LONDON

Year:	1603	1625	1665
Estimated population:	250,000	320,000	460,000
Plague deaths:	30,578	41,313	68,596

Did the disease disappear after 1351?

Plague came back regularly for another 300 years, especially in warm summers. Its worst effects were in seventeenth-century London where there was the greatest concentration of people. The most severe outbreak, in 1665, was known as the 'Great Plague of London'.

How was the plague spread?

The disease was caused by a bacterium living in blood. It was passed on by bites from the blood-sucking fleas of the black rat. This rat tended to live in houses, in close contact with people, and in the holds of ships. It was a ship which first brought the disease to England, arriving at the port of Melcombe in Dorset in June 1348.

To try to escape the plague some people whipped themselves to show God that they were sorry for their sins.

RED CROSS

In 1665 the London authorities tried to fight the plague by keeping victims apart from healthy people. They were shut up in their houses with their families, and food and drink were passed in to them. A red cross was painted on the door to warn healthy people to stay away.

Why did people whip themselves in plague time?

Many people thought that the disease was a punishment sent by God for sins they had committed. They tried to escape the punishment by showing God that they were truly sorry. They went on processions through the streets or towns – weeping, praying and lashing themselves with whips.

What was the Great Fire of London?

For almost five days in September 1666, a terrible fire raged across London. Four-fifths of the city was destroyed, including 87 churches and more than 13,000 houses. Altogether 100,000 people lost their homes.

The Great Fire of London began in a baker's shop in Pudding Lane.

Why was London a fire risk?

Most of the buildings of London were made of wood, because brick and stone were expensive. Land in the city was scarce so buildings were put up close together, separated only by narrow streets. As a result, when a fire started in one building, it spread easily to neighbouring homes.

How did the Great Fire of London start?

The fire started in a bakery in Pudding Lane, just north-east of London Bridge. The baker, Thomas Farynor, had failed to put out the fire in one of his ovens. Sparks landed on some stacked firewood, setting it alight.

FIRE BRIGADE

To reduce the risk of future fires, regulations were introduced calling for all new buildings to be made of brick or stone. New insurance companies were set up, which would pay for fire damage to the homes of people who took out policies. The insurance companies employed professional firefighters, in the hope of reducing fire damage. This was the beginning of the fire brigade.

The Great Fire rages through the city of London.

What caused the fire to spread so quickly?

The summer of 1666 was hot and rainless, and the dried-out timber buildings caught fire more easily than usual. The fire was fanned by a strong and steady east wind, which carried it west and down to warehouses by the river. These were full of goods which burned readily, such as oil, timber, hay, spirits and coal.

How did people try to fight the fire?

People used buckets of water and 'hand-squirts', which worked like bicycle pumps, squirting water at the fire. Unfortunately, there was a water shortage due to the dry summer, and water levels in wells and streams, where most people got their water, were very low.

What was a 'fire break'?

The best way to fight the fire was to destroy the buildings in its path, making a space called a 'fire break'. The houses were blown up with gunpowder, or pulled down with long hooks on poles. However, Lord Mayor Bloodworth, who was in charge of fighting the fire, could not bring himself to order this. He kept saying, 'Who will pay for the rebuilding?'

How many people died in the fire?

Amazingly, only six people are known to have died directly as a result of the fire. They included the maid in the bakery where the blaze started.

Why did the fire burn out?

The main reason was that the wind dropped and changed direction, blowing to the south towards the River Thames. Here, the fire burned out.

How did people explain the disaster?

Many thought that the fire must have been started by foreign enemies. Rumours spread that Frenchmen were seen putting 'fireballs' into houses. One Frenchman was almost killed because he was found carrying a box of tennis balls.

Who blamed God?

Another idea was that the fire had been sent by God, like the plague, as a punishment for sin. One preacher said that the fire was God's punishment on Londoners for being too greedy. His evidence was that 'the fire began in Pudding Lane and ended in Pie Corner'.

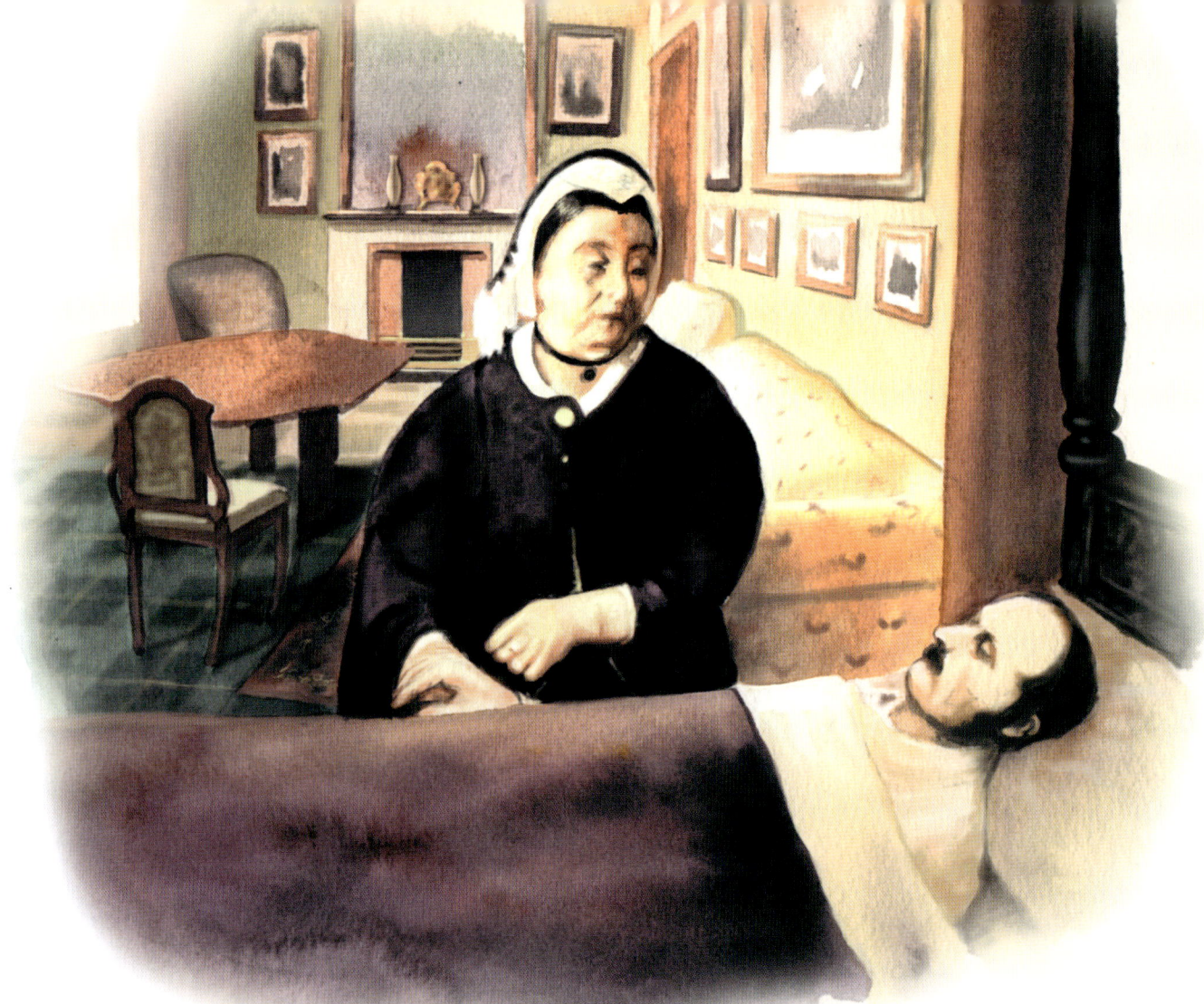

Queen Victoria sits at the bedside of her husband, who later died from typhoid.

What is typhoid?

Typhoid is a fever caused by a bacterium, which some people can carry without showing any symptoms. Typhoid carriers who prepare meals without washing their hands can pass on the disease to anyone who eats the food they have prepared. Prince Albert, the husband of Queen Victoria, died of typhoid fever in 1861.

Which disease was more deadly than bullets?

In wartime typhoid was a very common disease among soldiers, who caught it by drinking water polluted with sewage. During the South African Boer War of 1900-1, 6,425 British soldiers died from gunfire, while 42,741 caught typhoid, and 11,237 died of it.

Why was cold air bad for sweating sickness?

People who described the disease wrote that sufferers who drank anything cold, or allowed cold air on their bodies, died quickly. Those who wrapped up well were more likely to survive. It was probably caused by a virus, and may have been a form of flu.

PANDEMIC

A pandemic is a disease which strikes everywhere. In 1918-19, a deadly form of influenza raced around the world, killing between 20,000,000 and 30,000,000 people. In Britain the disease killed almost 200,000 individuals. The terrible thing about this virus was that it targeted mainly young people, below the age of 30. It is likely that the old had already come into contact with an earlier, less deadly, form of the same virus and had built up resistance to it.

What is a virus?

A virus is the simplest and smallest known living thing. Unlike bacteria, viruses can only exist inside the cells of other creatures. They take over a cell, and force it to make copies of the virus. The damage they do in the process causes many different diseases, including colds, flu (influenza), measles, mumps, chickenpox and smallpox.

What was an ague?

Ague was the English name for malaria, a fever-causing disease of the blood. The disease is passed on by the bite of a mosquito. It is almost unknown in Britain today, but it used to be common in low-lying wetlands where mosquitoes lived. These areas included the fens of East Anglia, the Somerset levels and the marshes of Kent and Essex.

What was the sweating sickness?

The sweating sickness was a mysterious disease that first appeared in Britain in 1485, and returned in 1508, 1517, 1528 and 1551. Its symptoms were fever with great sweating and burning thirst. It came on very suddenly, and death often followed in six hours.

How did malaria and influenza get their names?

'Malaria' is Italian for 'bad air'. People thought that malaria was caused by the bad air of the swamps where the disease was common. 'Influenza' is Italian for 'influence'. It was thought that flu was caused by the influence of the moon and stars.

What is a fever?

A fever is an abnormally high body temperature, often accompanied by violent shivering, sweating and a very fast pulse rate. This happens when the brain loses its ability to control our body temperature. Fevers can be a symptom of several different diseases, including malaria, influenza, typhoid and the 'sweating sickness'.

A Tudor noble suffering from the sweating sickness has more blankets brought to him by his servant.

John Snow studies his map, hoping to find a pattern to the cholera deaths in an area of London.

What is cholera?

Cholera is a deadly disease which causes an agonising death, after hours of continual vomiting and diarrhoea. Common in India for hundreds of years, the disease first reached Britain in 1831, when it was carried on trading ships. Four terrible outbreaks followed, with most of the victims in London.

When was water not fit to drink?

Andrew Borde, a sixteenth-century doctor, wrote, 'Water is not wholesome by itself for an Englishman. I myself, who am a physician, avoid water and take to good ale'. Until recently, most British people would have agreed. Even small children preferred the taste of ale or beer to the dirty drinking water available.

Why was water unhealthy in towns?

Water in towns was often polluted with sewage from toilets. Sewage is full of bacteria which can cause diseases like cholera and typhoid. It can also pass on the eggs of worms, which hatch out and breed inside people's stomachs.

Why was the River Thames a health risk?

By the middle of the nineteenth century, around 400 million litres of sewage poured straight into the River Thames every day. The water companies, which supplied water to street pumps, drew it all from the river. Not surprisingly, people who used this water for drinking, cooking and washing came down with many diseases.

What did people think caused cholera?

The commonest idea among doctors was that cholera was caused by a 'miasma', or unhealthy gas from rotting matter. Like many diseases, cholera was at its worst in the summer, when the streets of London were full of rotting rubbish and smelled horrible.

CHOLERA DEATHS IN LONDON

1831: about 6,000
1848-9: about 14,000
1854: 10,675
1866: about 5,000

How was the true cause of cholera discovered?

A London doctor called John Snow, believed that the 'miasma' idea did not fit the facts. Although everybody in a street breathed the same smelly air, they did not all catch cholera. Snow believed that the water supply was to blame.

THE 'GREAT STINK'

The 'Great Stink' was a nickname given to the hot summer of 1858, when the Thames stank so badly of sewage that Parliament had to close. To solve the problem a civil engineer, called Joseph Bazalgette, was employed to build a network of sewers that took the sewage away from the city. As the sewage disappeared, so did the threat of cholera.

How did Snow test his idea?

Between August 31 and September 9, 1848, almost 500 people died from cholera in a tiny area of central London. John Snow visited the district, questioning locals about where they got their drinking water. He came to suspect that one pump in Broad Street was to blame. He wrote, 'I found that nearly all the deaths had taken place within a short distance of the pump'.

Who didn't catch the disease?

Snow learned that none of the workers in the Broad Street brewery, at the centre of the outbreak, had come down with cholera. The reason was that they did not drink water, because the brewery gave them all a free daily supply of beer. This was more evidence that Snow's theory was right.

How did Snow end the outbreak?

Snow advised the local authorities to remove the handle from the Broad Street pump. Although they doubted his theory, they agreed and no more people died of cholera in the area.

Londoners in a beer tavern. Snow's survey of cholera sufferers in London showed that those who drank beer rather than water tended not to catch cholera.

Why did explosions happen in mines?

Coal gives off a highly explosive gas, called methane or fire damp, which collects in pockets underground. It is very hard to detect because it is invisible and odourless, and it can be set off by the slightest spark.

Why did mining disasters grow worse in the late 1880s?

In the 1800s most coal mines were small, employing not many more than 100 people. As the demand for coal increased pits were dug deeper, with longer tunnels and far more miners working in them. The worst mining disaster before 1850 killed 102 men. It happened in 1835 at Wallsend in Northumbria. The worst mining disaster in the second half of the century occurred in 1866, when 361 miners were killed at the Oaks Colliery at Barnsley in Yorkshire.

Why was the miners' job so important?

Britain's wealth was founded on coal power. In the nineteenth century it drove the machines in the factories of the new industrial towns, such as Manchester and Leeds. Coal was also used to heat homes and buildings. It powered the engines in trains and ships, and it was converted into gas and, later, electricity, to light streets and houses.

What was the most dangerous job?

Between the 1700s and 1900s no British job was harder or more dangerous than coal mining. Every year hundreds of miners were killed in explosions, rock-falls and underground flooding. Miners who survived into old age often fell ill with diseases caused by their work.

What was the worst British mining disaster?

On October 14, 1913, there was a massive explosion in the Universal coal mine at Senghenydd, in Wales. At the time almost 1,000 miners were working underground. Rescuers were able to save 498 of them, but fires stopped them from reaching the rest. After four days the rescuers gave up trying to find them, and to prevent further explosions they sealed off the mine. Four hundred and thirty nine miners lost their lives, leaving behind hundreds of widows and orphans.

Canaries sat in cages like this in the depths of the mine.

Miners shield their eyes from an explosion further along the pit.

Why did miners take canaries underground?

Miners began to take caged canaries underground in the nineteenth century. These little birds are much more sensitive to methane and carbon monoxide than people. A miner's canary would fall off its perch when gas was present, warning the miners to stop their work and leave the mine.

What is chokedamp?

Chokedamp was a name miners gave to carbon monoxide, another deadly but odourless gas given off by coal. Carbon monoxide kills by poisoning anyone who breathes it in.

BLACK LUNG DISEASE

Over their working lives miners continually breathe in particles of coal dust. These damage the lungs, causing thousands of tiny scars. As the scars build up, the men begin to suffer from pneumoconiosis, or black lung disease. Its symptoms are breathlessness and a constant cough. Sufferers are also more likely to develop other lung complaints, such as bronchitis. In the twentieth century this disease killed around 850 retired miners a year.

A Victorian family in a city slum.

How did smogs kill?

Smoky fogs were fatal to people who already had weakened lungs, from diseases such as tuberculosis (TB). This was a major killer in the cities of 1800s Britain. It is caused by a bacterium almost identical to the one which causes leprosy. The difference is that TB is much easier to catch. It is a disease which slowly destroys the sufferer's lungs.

Why did TB spread in slums?

The TB bacterium is killed by fresh air and sunlight, and survives best in dark, damp places. It is spread by coughing, and so it is most easy to catch in overcrowded places. Nowhere was more dark, damp and overcrowded than the slums of Victorian cities, so TB was common among the poor.

What was a 'pea souper'?

By the 1800s, thick and foul-smelling smoky fogs were a regular feature of the streets of London. They were called 'pea soupers' because they were a dirty yellow colour, unlike the usual white colour of fog. The smogs were even worse in the cities of northern Britain, where factory chimneys belched out poisonous smoke and turned all the walls of buildings black.

How can the air be dangerous?

From the seventeenth century, coal replaced wood as the main fuel burned in towns and cities. When coal burns it produces black smoke which contains poisonous sulphur dioxide. Foggy weather can prevent this smoke from escaping, causing deadly smogs.

What did the government do to stop the smog?

Clean Air acts were passed in 1956 and 1968. These banned the burning of coal in cities, calling for businesses and homes to switch to smoke-free fuels, such as gas.

Who first described a London smog?

In 1661, the writer John Evelyn wrote a book called *Fumifugium*, complaining that the 'glorious and ancient city' was now wrapping 'her stately head in clouds of smoke and sulphur'. He called for businesses burning coal to be banished from the city.

What are bronchitis and pneumonia?

Our lungs are made up of thousands of air passages, with tiny air pockets lower down. Bronchitis is a condition where the air passages become inflamed and swollen due to an infection. With pneumonia, it is the air pockets which become inflamed and fill up with water. Both can kill.

What was the 'Great Smog' of 1952?

Between Friday December 5 and Tuesday December 9, 1952, a thick smog covered London. It was so bad that all road, train and air transport was halted. Smog even found its way into London's theatres, and people sitting in the balcony of the Royal Festival Hall were unable to see the stage. Around 4,000 Londoners died as a result, mostly from bronchitis and pneumonia.

CLEAN AIR?

Our air looks cleaner, but it is still polluted by the millions of cars on our roads. Cars give off exhaust fumes, containing invisible poisonous gases, such as carbon monoxide, nitrogen dioxide and benzine. Bronchitis and pneumonia are still big killers and while TB is very rare today, there has been a massive increase in another lung complaint, asthma.

Londoners wait for a bus in a pea souper. One man holds a handkerchief to his mouth to stop him from breathing in the yellow smog.

Kings and Queens

Who was Boudicca?

Around two thousand years ago, Britain was divided between various tribes who all had their own leaders, and these tribes were split into two peoples. In the north and the west, there were the remnants of a people called the Picts. Everywhere else were the Celts, fiery people who also lived in France and Spain. They were divided into various groups who often fought each other over land and possessions. One of these Celtic tribes was called the Iceni. Their home was in present-day East Anglia, and in AD 60 Boudicca was their queen.

PROBLEM CHIEFTAIN

The great British chieftain Caractacus was a major problem for the conquering Romans. He kept attacking their legions. In AD 50, the Romans defeated him, and Caractacus was taken to Rome and paraded in front of the jeering crowds. It is said that when he saw the magnificent buildings of Rome, he exclaimed: 'I wonder that the Romans, who possess such palaces, should envy the huts of the Britons.'

Did the Celts have a religion?

The early Britons believed in a religion called Druidism. It was based on respecting nature. The Druids believed that many places were sacred, including woods, forests, groves and springs. During one of their rituals, they would cut mistletoe from a sacred oak tree with a golden sickle. The Druids are believed to have conducted ceremonies at Stonehenge, the circle of enormous and ancient stones on Salisbury Plain in Wiltshire.

Why did Boudicca become famous?

When Boudicca's husband, King Prasutagus died in either AD 59 or 60, he left all his wealth to his two daughters and half his kingdom to his wife. The other half of the estate went to the Romans who had just conquered Britain. But this did not satisfy the Romans and they looted Boudicca's palace, took her land, and flogged the queen in front of her family and servants.

Did Boudicca fight the Romans?

Yes, she gathered a vast army of Britons and, probably in AD 61, went on the attack, determined to drive the Romans out of Britain. Soon, she had wiped out the settlements of Colchester, London and St Albans, all Roman strongholds. But the Romans fought back with an army of 10,000 men and Boudicca's army was defeated somewhere near where Warwickshire is today. Boudicca herself escaped but she later committed suicide by taking poison.

What was Boudicca's Britain like?

In the time of the Celts, Britain was full of marshes and huge, dark forests. In between the long lines of rolling hills, were large clearings where people cultivated food and built small villages. The Romans, however, started building roads and towns that later grew into many of the cities that we have today.

What did Boudicca look like?

Early descriptions tell us that she was terrifying to look at. Very tall and strong, she had a mass of long hair that came down to her waist. According to the Roman writer Dio Cassius, it was bright red and often decorated with woad, a blue dye made from plants. During battles, she used to ride a chariot drawn by horses. She had a very loud voice, which people could hear over the din of battle.

Where is Queen Boudicca buried?

Legend has it that Boudicca's followers buried her body in a secret place where the Romans could not find it. It is said that her grave lies under Platform 8 at King's Cross Station in London. Of course, no one knows for sure. The Iceni might have taken Boudicca's body back to their land in East Anglia.

Did the Iceni take trophies when they attacked?

The Celts loved taking the heads of their enemies as trophies. They hung them up on temples, houses and gates. Numerous skulls have been found in the Walbrook, a river that used to run through London. They had probably been thrown there as offerings by Boudicca and her people when they sacked the city.

The warrior-queen, Boudicca, drives her horses on to face the Romans in battle.

BURNING THE CAKES

An ancient legend tells how King Alfred stumbled into a swineherd's cottage. The swineherd's wife, who did not recognize the king, said he could stay if he looked after the cakes she was baking while she went out. Some time later, the woman returned home to find Alfred dozing by the fire and the cakes burnt. She was about to tell him off when her husband turned up and recognized the king.

Was there a Roman king of Britain?

No. In Roman times, Britain was just a province and it was ruled by the Roman emperor from Rome. But by the beginning of the fifth century AD, the Roman Empire was falling apart. Most of the Roman soldiers in Britain were needed to defend their empire against the German tribes of central Europe. In 410, the last Roman soldiers left Britain, and by the end of the sixth century, the Roman occupation was a distant memory.

Who ruled Britain after the Romans left?

With the Romans gone, new invaders took over England. They were the Anglo-Saxons and they came from Germany. After landing in bands and settling in eastern and southern Britain, the Anglo-Saxons set up various kingdoms around the country, including Northumbria in the north, East Anglia in the east, Mercia in central England and Wessex, Essex, Sussex and Kent in the south. Each kingdom had its own ruler.

Did the Saxons get on well with each other?

No sooner had the Anglo-Saxons settled in Britain than they started fighting amongst themselves. Every so often, one kingdom would become bigger than the others and its king would call himself the king of the English. By 627, for example, King Edwin of Northumbria was so powerful that many recognized him as 'ruler of Britain'. Just five years later, in 632, the people of Mercia staged an attack on the Northumbrians. In 757, King Offa became ruler of all England. He treated the kingdoms outside Mercia as mere provinces.

Did the English live in peace under King Offa?

No. In 787, Viking ships were seen off the coast of England. It was the start of a sequence of raids that, by the middle of the ninth century, saw huge parts of Britain under Viking attack. Danes started settling in England until they had taken over the eastern part of the land and turned it into a kingdom called the Danelaw. From here they carried out raids on the neighbouring Saxon kingdoms. They kept on conquering until they came up against the only man in the country who could defeat them – Alfred the Great, king of Wessex.

How did Alfred beat the Vikings?

Alfred the Great.

By 871, it seemed that the kingdom of Wessex was going to be conquered by Danes led by their merciless leader Guthrum. Alfred's father, Ethelwulf, and all of Alfred's brothers were dead. Still a young man, Alfred was forced to hide in a swamp in Athelney in Somerset. From there, he organized one raid after another until he conquered the Vikings at the Battle of Edington in 878.

Did Alfred like being a warrior?

Alfred much preferred peace to war. He spent a lot of time praying and he rebuilt many churches that had been destroyed by the Vikings. He also spent a lot of time translating books. When no teachers could be found to teach children in England, he sent abroad for educated monks.

Who benefited from Alfred's reforms?

Alfred the Great spent the last twenty years of his life making England a safe place to live in. He built many new towns on the ruins of old Roman cities, and erected a large number of forts. Alfred also reorganized the army, which remained on duty even in harvest time when all able-bodied men were out in the fields.

Did Alfred banish the Vikings from England?

No, he had to make a treaty with Guthrum. The Vikings promised not to invade the kingdom of Wessex. In return, Alfred had to accept that Guthrum was the rightful ruler of the Danelaw. For a while, both parties lived in an uneasy alliance. But the Vikings would not give up their dreams of ruling the whole of England.

Viking ships approach the coast of England.

Did the Vikings ever conquer the whole of England?

After Alfred the Great died in 899, his successors began to win parts of England back from the Vikings, and regained control of much of the country. In 978, Vikings from Denmark started attacking England again. Now there was no great king like Alfred to hold them at bay. By 1016, a Danish king called Cnut was sitting on the English throne. He ruled over England, Denmark and Norway at the same time.

Was King Cnut really called that?

Yes, but English historians changed the name to Canute to make it sound more English. People did not like the idea that Canute was a Viking, and it was easier for them to think of him as English if he had a name they could pronounce.

Did becoming a king change Cnut?

In his youth King Cnut was known for his ferocious courage. His father, the Danish king Svein Forkbeard, had taught his son all about Viking pillaging and looting. But when he became king of England, Cnut learnt very quickly to listen to the earls and advisors at court as they were older and wiser than him. He brought security and justice to England, and was said to have become more English than the English!

Was Cnut a good king?

Cnut put his pillaging background behind him to become a good king. He worked hard to spread learning through his kingdom, and England became prosperous under his rule. Cnut also became a devout Christian and made a long pilgrimage to Rome to meet the Pope and ask forgiveness for killing people during his battles.

Did Cnut really stop the sea?

Legend has it that King Cnut's subjects kept showering him with praise and telling him how powerful he was. Some even insisted that the sea would obey his every command. The king promptly had his throne carried to the seashore. There he ordered the tide to withdraw. Needless to say, the sea did not obey and King Cnut was drenched. The wise ruler had made his point. No man was as powerful as God or nature.

King Cnut commands the sea to withdraw.

Lady Godiva prepares to ride around the city of Coventry.

Were the Vikings scared of anything?

Very few people have been able to match the Vikings' fierceness. When attacking a coastal settlement, they killed everyone they met, including babies and children. But even the bravest Viking warrior was afraid of ghosts. The merest hint of a white shape glowing in the dark would petrify a Viking. He would think that his dead ancestors had come to fetch him to the land of the dead.

LADY GODIVA

One of Cnut's earls, a Dane called Leofric, imposed heavy taxes on the people of Coventry. His Saxon wife, Lady Godiva, objected and made him a very special bet. She promised to ride around Coventry naked. If the people stayed in behind closed doors and did not peep at her, Leofric must reduce the taxes. But if just one person took a peek, the taxes stayed. Next day, Lady Godiva rode around naked. Nobody peeked, and the taxes were reduced.

Why was Harold known as Harefoot?

In 1037, Cnut was succeeded as king of England by his son Harold. He was known as Harefoot, because he could run as fast as a hare. His running was better than his ruling though, and he was a much poorer king than his father.

Who dug up his brother's body?

Cnut had another son, named Hardicnut, who was furious when Harefoot inherited the throne. So he invaded England in 1040, only to find that his brother had already died! Hardicnut took his revenge anyway, by digging up his brother's body and throwing it into a marsh.

Who died at a wedding?

Hardicnut was an unpopular king and the English were delighted that his reign lasted only two years. He died after having a fit while proposing the toast at a wedding.

Was England peaceful when Harold was king?

Harold had not been king for long when a Viking king called Hardrada invaded the north of England. With him was Harold's own brother Tostig, who had been exiled from England. Harold and his army marched north and killed both Hardrada and Tostig and most of their men at the Battle of Stamford Bridge.

How did Harold celebrate his victory over the Vikings?

Just as Harold and his men started celebrating their victory over Hardrada and Tostig, they received devastating news. William of Normandy and his men were sailing to England, determined to snatch the crown from Harold. Their ships had already left France and the wind was in their favour. They would reach the shores of England in a few days.

ROYAL HUMOUR

When King Hardrada once joked that Harold II would soon be forced to hand over a big part of England, Harold replied, 'I'll only give you six feet.' Then he looked the Viking up and down and added, 'No, seven, seeing as you're taller than most men.' Not long afterwards, Hardrada was killed in battle. His grave was about seven feet long.

Why did Halley's Comet appear in 1066?

Harold Godwinsson was the son of Godwin, the powerful Earl of Wessex, who had been advisor to King Edward the Confessor. When Edward died in 1066, Harold was crowned as the new king of England. William of Normandy was furious. He had grown up with Edward, and had received a promise from him that he would be the next king. William had also been made a promise by Harold. When he was shipwrecked in France, Harold had sworn to support William's claim to the English crown. When Halley's Comet rocketed across the sky in 1066, people believed it was a sign that God was angry at the breaking of these two promises.

What did Harold do when he heard that the Normans were about to invade England?

He turned his army round and started marching south right away. He reached London on October 5, and let his men have a well earned rest. Locals provided the army with food while Harold gathered reinforcements. But he knew that his men were too weary to fight another battle.

King Harold.

When did William of Normandy reach England?

William's forces landed at Pevensey on September 28, 1066. They were well prepared to fight the English. They rode on horseback and their favourite weapon was the lance. Some of the soldiers also used maces, which were heavy clubs with an iron head. Others in the army were skilled with the sword or longbow.

How do we know what happened at the Battle of Hastings?

The Battle of Hastings is shown in a famous work of art called the Bayeux Tapestry. Embroidered on bleached linen, it shows not only the battle but the preparations for it. It also shows the English retreating in defeat from Hastings, and Harold being killed. The last part is missing. Perhaps it was never completed. Experts think the tapestry was made in Winchester, England, for Odo, the bishop of Bayeux. He was William of Normandy's half-brother and helped plan the invasion of England.

What kind of weapons did Harold's army use?

Harold's army was made up mostly of foot-soldiers. They used heavy axes which they had to wield with both hands. As long as they stayed high up on a hill, there was not much the Normans or any other enemy could do to defeat them.

Where did Harold's forces meet William the Conqueror's army?

The two forces clashed near Hastings on October 14. The English fought bravely, forced the Normans to retreat and then chased after them. But the Normans then turned and broke through the English 'wall of shields'. Harold was wounded and quickly died. Some say he was shot in the eye by an archer; others that he was dragged down from his horse and lanced. William of Normandy was the new king.

King Harold is injured as an arrow hits him directly in the eye.

When did William become the king of England?

After winning the battle of Hastings, William made his way to London. On the way there, his men looted and pillaged farms and estates. On Christmas Day 1066, William was crowned king of England. The ceremony took place in the newly built Westminster Abbey. He became known as William the Conqueror.

Did William the Conqueror speak English?

He spoke French, as did his followers the Normans. They believed that French culture was the most advanced in Europe, looked down on the English language and were disgusted at the thought of having to speak in such a coarse tongue.

Did William the Conqueror's coronation go smoothly?

At one point during the coronation ceremony, the French noblemen heard shouting outside the abbey and thought that their new subjects were rebelling. In fact, the Archbishop of York was trying to get the English crowds to cheer. The French, fearing the worst, set fire to the buildings around the abbey and William was crowned to the acrid smell of burning.

How did William treat his Saxon enemies?

Immediately after the coronation, many Saxon earls and barons were stripped of their property and removed from positions of power. The land was taken from them and given to French noblemen. Anyone who showed hostility to the Normans lost all their belongings and their houses were burnt down. Even so, there were still many uprisings. In 1067, the people of Wales and Kent tried to rebel against the new king. Then, in 1070 and 1071, there were rebellions in the Midlands. But William the Conqueror crushed all opposition and by 1072 was the undisputed ruler of all England.

The king directs operations as yet another Norman castle is built.

PROTECTING THE HUNT

William the Conqueror loved hunting in his royal forests. No one else but him and the members of his court were allowed to hunt there. People who were caught stealing deer or other animals from the king's forests were fined or thrown into prison. Sometimes they had a hand chopped off or an eye gouged out. These measures did not scare everyone off. Some English people saw it as their duty to steal from a foreign king.

What is the Domesday Book?

William wanted to know exactly how much land everyone in England possessed so he could tax them. In December 1085, he decided to carry out a survey. Officials were sent all around the country to make records. All the details were put down in a book divided into two volumes. The English, unhappy about the fact that they were going to be charged more tax, dubbed it the Domesday Book. It still exists today, kept safe in the Public Record Office in London. It shows that the king owned 20 per cent of all the land in England. Another 25 per cent was owned by the Church, whilst an impressive 50 per cent was controlled by Norman barons. Only 5 per cent was in the hands of the English.

Did William change the way England was run?

The new king did not trust the English. He stripped the Church of its power and made his French friend Lanfranc the Archbishop of Canterbury. He claimed all the land in the country as his own. Then he leased it out to barons he trusted. The barons, or vassals as they were called, hired the land out to lords of the manors. And the lords hired parts of that land out to the poorer folk. The new king also built lots of castles, so that all this hiring out could be ruled over with an iron fist.

Did William build castles in London?

The Tower of London and Windsor Castle are perhaps the best known castles built by William the Conqueror. The part of the Tower of London built by him is known as the White Tower. Over the years, other kings added to the building.

How did the lords make money?

Corn was grown all over England and people had to take it to the mill where it was ground into flour. The mill belonged to the lord on whose land they lived and he charged them a share of the corn for using it. Sometimes the lord of the manor also owned the village oven and people had to pay him for using that too.

When did William die?

William spent the last years of his life fighting his enemies in Normandy. In 1086, he visited England for the last time. A year later, during a battle, his horse stumbled outside Rouen. The king was thrown to the ground, and six weeks later, on September 7, 1087, he died.

The two volumes of the Domesday Book.

ROBIN OF SHERWOOD

While Richard was away crusading, people in England suffered hardship. No one, it seemed, had any money left for food after taxes had been collected. A few brave souls took to the forests, poaching from the king's lands and stealing from the rich as they passed from one baron's estate to another. The exploits of these unknown men gave rise to the legend of Robin Hood and the outlaws of Sherwood Forest.

The legendary outlaw, Robin Hood.

Who was Richard the Lionheart's mother?

She was a lady called Eleanor of Aquitaine, and Richard was her favourite son. She taught him music and poetry, and encouraged him to learn as many languages as possible. Richard learnt a good number, but he never spoke English at all. When he grew up and the Christian princes were preparing for the Crusades, Eleanor was often overheard boasting how her Richard was the 'great one and the good'.

Who threatened to sell the city of London?

Even before he became king, Richard had decided to go off and fight in the Third Crusade. He raised money through taxes and by selling off some of the Crown's assets. At one point he even threatened to sell the city of London if he could get a good price for it. In December 1189, the same year he was crowned, he set off on the Crusades with Philip II of France and Frederick I of Germany.

What were the Crusades?

They were a series of holy wars fought between Muslims and Christians who both wanted to control the area that was known as Palestine, where Jesus had lived and died. The Holy Land was also sacred to Muslims, who had lived there since the 600s. Christian pilgrims wanted to be able to visit their holy places, such as the city of Jerusalem, now under the control of Muslim Turks who had stopped pilgrimages.

Who was Richard the Lionheart?

He was a distant relative of William the Conqueror. His father was Henry II of England, and Richard was born at Beaumont Palace near Oxford in England. As an adult, he was famous for his bravery, which earned him the nickname 'Coeur de Lion' or Lionheart. His dedication to the Christian faith and his love of poetry were unrivalled by any other king of the time. Not that he spent a great deal of time composing verses in England. During his ten-year reign, which began in 1189 after the death of his father, he only spent a total of six months on English soil.

Was Richard's campaign in the Holy Land successful?

Richard and Philip II of France managed to win the city of Acre, near Jerusalem, from the Muslims. But then the two kings quarrelled and Philip returned home, leaving Richard on his own. The king of England fought on but could not take Jerusalem from the Muslim ruler Saladin. Richard did manage, however, to negotiate a deal that allowed Christian pilgrims to visit the holy city without fear of persecution.

Who was Saladin?

He was a fierce and very intelligent warrior. As fiercely Muslim as Richard the Lionheart was Christian, he built mosques and universities and encouraged writers to write about Islam and the holy wars against Christian kings like Richard. Under his rule, the Muslim countries of the eastern Mediterranean flourished.

What happened to Richard on the way home?

On his way home from the Crusades, Richard's ship was caught in a storm and wrecked in the Adriatic Sea. Richard donned a disguise and tried to travel home through the lands of his enemies in Austria, but was captured. His mother, Queen Eleanor, had to raise a hefty ransom for the king's release. The money was collected from the people, and in early 1194 Richard was released and returned home.

How did Richard the Lionheart die?

Soon after he had returned from the Crusades, Richard was off on his travels again. He sailed to France to collect money from the good people of Chalus, who had found treasure on his land. While laying siege to a castle, Richard was struck in the shoulder by an arrow. The wound refused to heal, and in April 1199 he died. Richard was buried in Fontevrault, and the lion-hearted king's heart was given as a gift to the cathedral of Rouen.

King John commands his soldiers to rescue his ill-gotten treasure from the Wash.

Who was John the Bad?

John was Richard the Lionheart's youngest brother. He was the only one of Henry II's sons who had been left with no land to rule after his father's death, which led to people calling him John Lackland. While Richard was missing in Austria on his way home from the Crusades, John plotted to prevent the king ever returning home. He wanted the throne for himself. During this time, he encouraged the barons of the country to disobey Richard.

How much did John the Bad like treasure?

John was famous for his love of magnificent clothes, sumptuous feasts, and especially treasure. By the end of his reign he was fighting with his own barons, and a well known story tells how the king tried to carry the treasures he had stolen from them across the Wash. The tide came in and all the treasures were washed away, leaving King John heartbroken. He died shortly afterwards.

Did Richard the Lionheart forgive his brother when he returned from the Crusades?

When Richard the Lionheart returned from the Crusades, he forgave John for trying to steal his throne. He genuinely believed that his younger brother had been led astray by the crafty barons and the people at court. When Richard died, John inherited the throne at last, and became the king of England.

Why was John called the Bad?

While John was on the throne, the French managed to win back their land in Normandy, Maine and Anjou from the English. John was forced into war to try to win them back. To pay for his armies, he had to tax his people. When the battles went badly for him, the king returned to England defeated and poor. He then had to command his people to pay even heavier taxes. This did nothing to improve his popularity. People thought that, compared to his brother Richard, he was not much of a king.

Did the Pope think King John was bad?

King John even incurred the anger of the Pope, by refusing the Pope's nomination of a cardinal named Stephen Langton as the next Archbishop of Canterbury. When John offered the office to one of his own favourites instead, the Pope shut down all the churches in England. John reacted by stealing some of the Church's treasures. The Pope then had him excommunicated – in other words, thrown out of the Church.

Did anyone try to rebel against King John?

Most ordinary people had no choice but to pay the heavy taxes demanded by the king. But the barons had the power to fight back. In 1215, they rebelled against their king. At the end of the uprising, in a meadow at Runnymede on the south bank of the Thames, John was forced to sign a document called the Magna Carta.

WANDERING MINSTREL

Popular legend has it that a wandering minstrel called Blondel went off in search of Richard the Lionheart when he was held captive in Austria. One day, the minstrel heard a familiar song drifting out of a tower window. Could it be the king? Blondel started singing the words and the prisoner in the tower answered. Blondel informed the local monks, who quickly sent word to England. Soon the English were raising money for the king's ransom.

The Magna Carta.

What was the Magna Carta?

It was a special document that guaranteed people certain rights to protect them from greedy kings. Barons could not be taxed without their consent. People were protected from corrupt officials who were always trying to demand more tax. Freemen could not be arrested, tried and imprisoned by anyone except a jury. At the time, the Magna Carta did not mean much to ordinary people, but it became the basis of many rights that we all enjoy today.

Who dug up the body of bad King John?

King John died in 1216, still as unpopular as when he had inherited the throne of England from his brother Richard. His nine-year-old son, Henry III, inherited the throne. Henry never forgot his father. When he grew up, he decided that Westminster Abbey was not grand enough for grand kings like him. So he had it rebuilt. Then he dug up the body of John the Bad and had it reburied in a magnificent new grave.

What were the Wars of the Roses?

Beginning in 1455, the English families known as the houses of York and Lancaster fought for the English crown. Their battles were called the Wars of the Roses, because the Yorkists' symbol was a white rose and the Lancastrians' a red one. By 1471, it seemed the house of York had a firm grip on the throne with the reign of Edward IV. The white rose appeared to have won. But the wars continued when, in April 1483, Edward died unexpectedly.

Who were the Woodvilles?

The older prince was named King Edward V, but because he was so young his uncle Richard was appointed his guardian or 'protector'. When the Woodville family, the relatives of Edward's mother Elizabeth Woodville, tried to gain influence with the young king, Richard took drastic action. He locked the two princes away in the Tower of London before Edward could be crowned. Then he took the throne himself, and was crowned as Richard III.

Did Edward IV have any heirs?

He had two sons, Edward and Richard, but they were still young when he died. Edward, the rightful heir to the throne, was thirteen and Richard was eleven.

Who was Richard III?

Richard III was the brother of Edward IV, and the uncle of the heirs to the throne, Edward and Richard. When the young princes disappeared, people were convinced that Richard had killed them. This has never been proved, but it has led to Richard being portrayed as one of the most evil of kings. Some historians wrote that he was destined to be evil when he was born with a full set of teeth!

Richard III is run through at the Battle of Bosworth.

Was Richard III a good or a bad king?

Before he was crowned, Richard was known as a just man who would not accept bribes. While governing some parts of England for his brother, Edward IV, he was known to help out the poor and the needy. He even got permission from his brother to hold fairs so that people could trade with their neighbours. As a king, he did more for the common people than any other ruler before him. He stopped all taxes on books and he made sure that all laws were written in English instead of Latin so that everyone could understand them. Richard also started a postal service and gave grants to poor students.

Richard III watches the two young princes sleeping in their quarters.

Was Richard III really a hunchback?

The politician Sir Thomas More and the famous playwright William Shakespeare both describe Richard as 'crookback' or 'crouchback', but they were writing years after his death. He is portrayed as a hunchback in Shakespearean plays, but this may just make it easier for audiences to identify him as a villain. He was certainly a very capable fighter, and was also known to be a very elegant dancer.

What were Richard III's last words?

At the Battle of Bosworth Field in August 1485, Richard found himself completely surrounded by the soldiers of Henry Tudor. Henry was descended from the house of Lancaster and wanted to win the throne back for the family of the red rose. A number of lords who Richard thought he could trust had betrayed him and joined Henry's army. Richard fought with incredible bravery, but when he was cut down the Wars of the Roses were over. His last words were: 'Treason! Treason! Treason!'

DEATH OF THE PRINCES

To this day, no one knows for certain if King Richard III was responsible for the deaths of the young princes Edward and Richard. In 1674, two skeletons were found in the Tower. Were they the bones of the missing boys? In the 1930s, the skeletons were examined by experts. They could not decide how old the bones were or whether they belonged to boys or girls. The mystery remained unsolved.

Where was Richard III buried?

After his death on the battlefield Richard III was not laid to rest in Westminster Abbey like many other kings. Instead, he was buried in a remote church. Some years later, vandals broke into his grave and stole the body. No one knows what happened to it.

Henry VIII practises his falconry techniques.

Who was Henry VIII?

Henry VIII was the son of Henry Tudor (Henry VII) who had defeated Richard III at the Battle of Bosworth Field. He was born on June 28, 1491. As he was the king's second son he did not expect to inherit the throne of England. But his elder brother Arthur died young. Henry was crowned in 1509 when he was just 18 years old.

LITTLE JACK HORNER

It is said that an abbot once sent Henry VIII twelve documents hidden in a pie. The documents made Henry the owner of twelve manors. But the messenger who carried the pie managed to sneak one document out from under the crust. It made him the owner of a house called the Manor of Mells in Somerset. The messenger's name was Little Jack Horner and he became famous when a nursery rhyme was written about how he found himself a 'plum' home.

Did the young Prince Henry go to school?

Like many rich people of his time, Henry had his own personal tutor. He was a priest called John Skelton. Henry's lessons included English, French, Latin, Arithmetic and Divinity. Henry was also very good at chess, an early form of tennis, bowls and martial arts. He also liked composing songs. As he grew older, Henry became rather fond of gambling, a pastime that he would enjoy for the rest of his life. He also jousted on horseback, and hunted with falcons. A lot of women were attracted to Henry, and it was no wonder. He was tall, handsome and sporty, and was heir to the throne of England.

What sports did ordinary people play?

When Henry became king, he forbade ordinary people to play sports such as football or games with cards or dice. He wanted everyone to concentrate on their work. In those days, people had to work 17 hours a day or more! The only sport that was allowed was archery, because Henry thought it might come in useful if people ever had to defend their country.

How much did Henry VIII enjoy his food?

Henry loved food with a passion, and ate huge meals. During a dinner held in honour of a French king, he and his guests ate 5,000 chickens and drank 25,000 litres of beer! At another meal, laid on by the Marquis of Exeter, Henry sampled stewed sparrows, pheasant, stork, heron, venison, roast chicken, gulls, rabbit and blancmange. All this feasting was, of course, not very good for the king's health. In later life he became obese and suffered from many diseases. He could no longer fit into his armour. Indeed, during the last five years of his reign, he could no longer stand up.

King Henry VIII lived in Hampton Court palace for many years.

How many times did Henry VIII marry?

He was married six times. His first wife was Catherine of Aragon, his brother's widow, who bore him a daughter, Mary. Henry separated from Catherine and married her maid of honour, Anne Boleyn, who also produced a daughter, Elizabeth. Desperate for a son, Henry had her beheaded for infidelity. Next came Jane Seymour who, in October 1537, gave birth to a boy, Edward. She died soon after, and Henry married Anne of Cleves. He divorced her for Catherine Howard. She followed poor Anne Boleyn to the block, before Henry finally married Catherine Parr.

HENRY'S SPECIAL FRIEND

Henry VIII had all manner of advisors at court to run his affairs and to keep him amused. One special servant had the rather daunting task of talking to the king when he was on the toilet. Popular topics would have included hunting, jousting, war and women. It was probably best not to talk about marriage!

Why did Henry argue with the Pope?

Henry wanted to make sure he had a son who would inherit the throne. When Henry's first wife, Catherine of Aragon failed to give birth to a healthy boy, he decided to divorce her and marry someone else. But the Pope refused to give Henry a divorce. So Henry declared himself head of the Christian Church in England and at the same time declared himself free of his wife.

What did Henry think of Anne of Cleves' portrait painter?

Not a lot. Anne had been recommended as a wife by Henry's advisor Thomas Cromwell. Henry had never laid eyes on her before the wedding, he had merely seen a portrait of her. When he did finally see her, she was not at all to his liking. The two soon got divorced and Henry married Catherine Howard. But he was soon convinced she was being unfaithful, so she was beheaded. Henry's last wife was a widow, Catherine Parr. She achieved the difficult feat of surviving Henry, who died on January 28,1547.

Who were Queen Elizabeth I's parents?

Elizabeth I was the daughter of King Henry VIII by his second wife, Anne Boleyn. She was born on September 7, 1533. As a child, she was only third in line to the throne. Her half-brother, Edward, the son of Jane Seymour, was king after Henry VIII but died at the age of 15. He was succeeded by Mary, the daughter of Catherine of Aragon, but in 1558 she also died. So Elizabeth became queen of England and was crowned on January 15, 1559.

How many times did Elizabeth marry?

Elizabeth was afraid that if she married, her husband would try to influence her decisions. Some of her favourite men at court included the dashing Robert Dudley, Christopher Hatton who was famous for his dancing, and Walter Raleigh, a soldier and explorer. Another close friend of the queen was Francis Drake, to whom she gave a magnificent sword with the words 'To my dear pyrate' carved on the handle. But despite having all these favourites, Elizabeth I never married.

Was Queen Elizabeth popular with her subjects?

Elizabeth was very popular. Everywhere she went, huge crowds gathered to cheer her. People thought up all sorts of magnificent names to call her, such as Gloriana, to show how glorious she was, and Virgin Queen, to show that she had dedicated her life to her people and not to a husband. The poet Edmund Spenser even wrote a poem about her called *The Faerie Queene*.

Was Elizabeth a happy child?

Elizabeth I had a very difficult childhood, which left her shy and insecure about her looks even as an adult. As a little girl, she was always being moved from one palace to another. Her father Henry VIII, who had wanted a boy, ignored her. Luckily, the young princess had a dedicated tutor called Kate Ashley. She encouraged her to learn Latin, Greek, French and Italian. Elizabeth was respected for her intelligence and energy. Even as an old woman she was vain about her appearance and never appeared in public without her wig, makeup and jewels.

English ships attack the Spanish Armada off the coast of England.

What kind of bed did wealthy Elizabethans like?

During Elizabeth I's reign people started to stuff their mattresses with feathers rather than straw. Four-poster beds were very popular, and people liked them so much that they left them to their descendants in their wills.

Did Elizabeth I ever visit her friends?

In a bid to stay in touch with the people of her land, Queen Elizabeth I went on what she called 'progresses'. During these she would stay with rich families while she toured the local area. These visits usually cost the hosts a great deal, often sending them into near-bankruptcy. Elizabeth would bring her whole court, servants and advisors with her. She even brought her own four-poster bed.

How did people cook in Elizabethan times?

Most people cooked their food over an open fire. Meat was roasted on a spit. Often, it was the job of the family dog to turn the spit. It would run round and round on a treadmill. People also baked food by putting it inside an iron box and then burying the box in the hot ashes of the fire.

What were houses like during Elizabethan times?

Up until Elizabethan times, houses were designed to keep people out so they looked more like castles than houses. In a time of prosperity, Elizabeth's subjects were not bothered about people attacking them, so they built houses with large windows that would let in a lot of light and also show off their furniture. They used wood rather than stones for building and had beautiful gardens, designed as places of rest and relaxation.

Queen Elizabeth studies her reflection in a mirror.

Did England prosper under Elizabeth?

When Elizabeth came to the throne in 1559, England was considered a poor country. Even the nobility were starved of cash. The new queen was to change all that. Under her, England was to become one of the most powerful and respected nations in the world. At home, the wool and weaving trades flourished, along with farming. English ships explored and traded overseas. Queen Elizabeth loved music, poetry and drama, so those became popular too. Geniuses like the playwrights Ben Jonson and William Shakespeare lived during her reign.

THE ARMADA

In 1588 King Philip II of Spain decided to conquer England and sent a fleet of 130 warships to invade. Elizabeth I fought back with 197 ships under the leadership of Howard of Effingham and Sir Francis Drake. While the Spanish Armada was moored in Calais, the English set fire to some of their own ships and sent them into the harbour to cause chaos. Many of the Spanish ships managed to escape the flames, but were caught in a storm and sunk. The invasion had failed.

Which queen was always ill?

Who was Queen Anne's husband?

Queen Anne was married to Prince George of Denmark. He was said to be rather a dull fellow who spent most of his time trying to solve mathematical puzzles.

The daughter of James II, Queen Anne was born on February 6, 1665. She was the last ruler of England from a family called the Stuarts. Anne reigned from 1702 to 1714. According to historians of the time she was very beautiful but a succession of illnesses left their mark on her. At the age of 12, she contracted smallpox, which left her with scars on her face. She also suffered from gout, an illness caused by eating too much rich food. As she grew older, Anne developed rheumatism. She also grew so fat that she had to be hoisted on to her throne. Queen Anne was also terribly short-sighted, and had to screw up her eyes to see properly. This made many people who saw her think she was frowning all the time.

Servants prepare to hoist Queen Anne on to her throne.

QUEEN ANNE'S REVENGE

Blackbeard was one of the most infamous pirates that ever lived. During Queen Anne's War he was a privateer, raiding for the queen. Then he turned to real piracy, keeping any treasure he looted just for himself. In 1717, he captured a French slave ship which he equipped with 40 cannons. He named his new pirate ship, *Queen Anne's Revenge*, in honour of his favourite queen who had died three years earlier. Blackbeard was finally cornered and killed in a fight with a navy ship. In modern times, the wreck of his *Queen Anne's Revenge* was rediscovered off the coast of North Carolina, USA.

Was Queen Anne a successful ruler?

Yes, she was a popular monarch, and people in Britain enjoyed relative peace and prosperity. During her reign, science and the arts were developing, and architecture and furniture became more elegant. In Europe, the Duke of Marlborough led British armies to victory in battles and British ships plied their trade to ports in faraway Africa and America. Colonies in America grew stronger too.

What were privateers?

Privateers were really pirate ships in disguise. Their owners and sailors would obtain a 'letter of marque' from their king or queen, giving them permission to attack and loot enemy ships. The sailors would then keep most of the treasure and pay a portion to their rulers. It was an economical way for kings and queens to increase their wealth as well as their power on the high seas. Queen Anne was very fond of using privateers.

What was Queen Anne's War?

Queen Anne's War was fought between England and France and started just before Anne came to power. The two European nations were fighting over which one of them should have control of large areas of land in Canada and America. At the end of the war, which lasted until 1713, Newfoundland and Nova Scotia became British territories. It was a big success for Queen Anne.

Who hunted from a chariot?

Like many other noblewomen of her time, Queen Anne took great delight in playing card games. She also enjoyed strolling around her gardens with friends. Her favourite beverage was tea, often drunk with a nip of gin in it to ease the pain of her various ailments. On occasion, the Queen also enjoyed hunting. But because of her rheumatism, she had to use a horse-drawn chariot instead of riding on a horse.

What is Queen Anne furniture?

It is a style of furniture that was popular during the reign of Queen Anne. Chairs, beds and desks had curved legs called 'cabriole' legs. Carpenters often made this kind of furniture using walnut, maple or cherry wood.

Did Queen Anne have any children?

Yes, she had seventeen children! But only one survived infancy. His name was William, Duke of Gloucester, and many people said he was destined for greatness. Unfortunately, he was no healthier than his mother, and died soon after his twelfth birthday. When Queen Anne herself died on August 1, 1714, the English throne passed to her German cousin, who became George I.

'Mad' King George

When did George III become king?

George III became King in 1760. He came from a family with roots in Germany but had spent all of his childhood in England. George was in fact very proud to be British. By the time he came to power, Britain had a government led by a prime minister. The king often did not see eye to eye with the prime minister and other politicians and did his best to press his own ideas of what should be done.

BETTER CONDITIONS

While George III was arguing with his politicians, the ordinary people were working to better their lot. A law was passed allowing people to strike if they were unhappy with their wages or their working conditions. Catholics were allowed to vote in elections for the first time, and the slave trade in England was finally abolished.

What kind of childhood did George III have?

George III is believed to have had a miserable childhood. Despised by both parents for being a weakling, he was often scolded by his mother and ignored by his father. He was prone to crying in front of guests, a habit which infuriated both his parents. As an adult, he also stuttered. King George quarrelled with his own servants, hated the trappings of royalty and preferred the simple things of life. He also showed an interest in new farming methods, which led people at court to call him Farmer George.

Did George III have a family of his own?

George married Charlotte Sophia in 1761. The couple were devoted to each other and had fifteen children, nine sons and six daughters. Family life was very important to George. He lavished a lot of time on his children and often took them on holiday to English seaside resorts.

Did George III really go mad?

Unfortunately, King George began suffering mental illness some time in the 1780s. People thought the stress of his country's many battles had been too much for him. Today, we know he suffered from a rare blood disease called porphyria.

What was the Boston Tea Party?

When George III was crowned king, America was still an English colony. But running America from across the Atlantic Ocean proved to be expensive. In 1767, the English parliament decided to tax the Americans, with the extra income to the government going to help police the colonies. The new law did not go down well in America. On December 16, 1773, some men in Boston refused to pay tax on a shipment of tea and threw it in the water. The incident was nicknamed the Boston Tea Party. A war erupted between England and her colonists in America. By July 4, 1776, the Americans had declared independence from Britain. George III was blamed for the loss of a valuable colony.

Did England and America make peace after the Tea Party?

British naval officers had the habit of kidnapping American sailors. They forced them to abandon their ships and serve in the English navy instead. This did not go down too well with the American government. In 1812 another war broke out between the two nations until the English promised not to hijack any more American sailors.

Did King George III carry on as king when he was mad?

He tried, but his son George, Prince of Wales, had to be made Regent in 1811. This meant he ruled in the king's place. The Prince Regent had a reputation as a lady's man. In 1785, he had secretly married a Catholic woman called Maria Fitzherbert. The British government did not accept the marriage and in 1795, the Prince Regent was married again, this time to Caroline of Brunswick. When George III died in 1820, the Prince Regent became king in his place. He was crowned George IV, but poor Caroline was not allowed to attend the coronation.

Settlers, dressed as Native Americans, empty crates of tea into the sea at Boston.

Was George IV a popular king?

The period when George IV ruled is known as the Regency period. It was not a happy time for many ordinary people. Twenty years of war with Napoleon had left many people penniless and out of work. There were food shortages and the prices of many things were beyond most workers' means. Despite all this, George IV lived in lavish splendour. He built the Royal Pavilion, a magnificent palace in Brighton where he used to spy on guests when they came for dinner.

What was George IV's favourite food?

The Prince Regent loved his food. His favourite foods for tea included regalia of cucumbers; calves' head pie; boiled rabbit; pigeon stew; whole pig slit down the back and boiled with herbs; stew of silver eel; buttered lobsters and bombarded veal. For dessert, he enjoyed calves' foot pudding with sliced almonds and lemon juice.

Queen Victoria and her
beloved Prince Albert.

When did Victoria become Britain's Queen?

On June 24, 1837, Princess Victoria was woken up early. Her uncle had died and she had become the new British queen. She was only 18 but she took her responsibilities seriously. At first she relied heavily on Lord Melbourne, the prime minister and leader of the ruling Whig party, for advice. But as she gained more confidence, she started to trust her own judgement in her work.

HARD WORK

In 1840, only 20 per cent of children went to school. The others had to work. The lucky ones were made apprentices and learnt a trade, while others became servants. Some poor children started working in coal-mines at the age of five and it was known for them to work 16 hours a day. During the Victorian age this was eventually cut down to ten hours for both children and adults.

When was Victoria born?

Queen Victoria was born on May 24, 1819. Her grandfather was King George III and her father was Prince Edward, Duke of Kent. Queen Victoria's mother was a beautiful German woman called Victoria of Saxe-Coburg. The young princess was christened Alexandrina Victoria. Her mother called her Victoria, but everyone else called her by her pet name, Drina.

Did Victoria have a happy childhood?

Queen Victoria had a very sheltered childhood. Her mother was scared that one of her relatives might try to assassinate her to stop her becoming ruler of Britain when her uncle, King William IV, died. So the princess was always watched over by guards, even during her lessons and especially when having meals. When she went up or down the stairs, someone always used to hold her hand, in case she was knocked over. Despite all this, Princess Victoria was a very happy and cheerful child.

Who did Victoria marry?

She married a German cousin of hers, called Prince Albert of Saxe-Coburg. In 1839, Albert visited Queen Victoria in England. She was very taken with him, but Albert was not so sure about his feelings or the idea of being married to the British queen. However, Victoria won him over and in time the pair became inseparable. They married in 1840, and had nine children.

Was Prince Albert popular with the British?

Some mistrusted Albert because he spoke English with a thick German accent. But Prince Albert worked very hard for the British people. He forced Victoria to think about social problems, and helped bring about a law to improve children's working conditions in factories. He also promoted British business, science and enterprise.

What made Victoria dress in black?

When Prince Albert died at the age of 42 on December 14, 1861, Queen Victoria was devastated. She locked herself away for nearly ten years, spending time in her country houses on the Isle of Wight and at Balmoral in Scotland. She still managed to do her duties, helped by her ministers. But the British people wanted to see their queen. The prime minister, Benjamin Disraeli, convinced her to start taking on public engagements again. She obeyed but from then on she always appeared in public dressed in black as a sign of mourning for her beloved Albert.

What did people do for fun in Victorian times?

They went to the theatre, read magazines called penny dreadfuls, and played in the park. In 1851, they could also go to a grand exhibition in the Crystal Palace in London. Among the exhibits were a 24-tonne block of coal, steam engines, railway trains, a fountain that sprayed French perfume, and an early version of the typewriter. Visitors to the Crystal Palace could also admire a huge diamond called the Koh-i-Noor. Today this diamond sits on top of the queen's crown. The exhibition showed how technology was changing life in Britain for the better, with many people having more to eat and living better lives.

Who had the first Christmas tree in Britain?

Queen Victoria and Prince Albert were the first people in England to have a Christmas tree, which up until then had been a German custom. They decorated it with pears, apples, walnuts and little figures. When pictures of the royal family and their tree appeared in magazines, the fashionable members of society rushed out to buy one. A new British tradition had been established.

Crystal Palace was built for the Great Exhibition of 1851.

When was Elizabeth II born?

Her Majesty the Queen was born Princess Elizabeth Alexandra Mary at 2.40 am on April 21, 1926 in her grandparents' house in London. She is the eldest daughter of King George VI and Queen Elizabeth, later Queen Mother. At the time of her birth, her grandfather George V was the king of the United Kingdom.

What was Elizabeth II like as a child?

The queen's parents were determined that she should have as normal a life as possible. She lived in the family home at No 145, Piccadilly and that was to be her home until her father became king in 1936. The world was changing and the royal family knew they had to change with it. They made sure that the little princess and her sister, Princess Margaret, would not grow up spoiled or not knowing what their duties to their country were.

Where did Elizabeth II go to school?

The Queen's mother had wanted her daughter to be educated at a public school, but royal tradition was for princesses to be taught at home. Elizabeth had private lessons at home. She was taught by a Scottish governess named Miss Crawford, or Crawfie as the princess called her.

What did Elizabeth II do during the Second World War?

During the Second World War, the young princesses Elizabeth and Margaret stayed at Windsor Castle where they sheltered from bombing in an air-raid shelter. They also travelled to Balmoral in Scotland, and Sandringham in Norfolk. There they helped local people gather in the harvest. At the age of 18, Princess Elizabeth joined the Auxiliary Territorial Services, and by the end of the war she had become a junior commander. Both princesses joined in the celebrations marking the end of the war. As no one recognized them, they took great delight in knocking people's hats off their heads!

Queen Elizabeth II's coronation in 1953.

Queen Elizabeth II as she looks today.

What does Queen Elizabeth do each day?

The queen is head of state and head of the Commonwealth. She opens parliament and signs Acts of Parliament. She and her family also promote Britain abroad. Every morning, the queen reads some of the 200 to 300 letters she receives each day. They are all answered by her staff. The queen also looks at papers sent to her by members of the government.

When did Elizabeth become queen?

Princess Elizabeth became queen on February 6, 1952 following the death of her father George VI. She was on a Commonwealth tour in Kenya, Africa, when she heard the news. She immediately returned to London, and was met at Heathrow airport by her uncle the Duke of Gloucester and the Prime Minister Winston Churchill. The queen was then crowned in Westminster Abbey on June 2, 1953. Many people bought television sets just so that they could watch the ceremony. It made the coronation the first great television event in the history of the world.

What kind of people does Elizabeth II meet?

The queen meets a number of important people, like ambassadors from other countries, Church officials and government ministers. She also goes out on public engagements, visiting hospitals, factories and schools. At 7.30 pm each evening, she receives a report from parliament. Then she might go to a film premiere, a concert or a party organized by one of her many charities. After that, she often works late into the night, looking at more government papers.

What are the queen's favourite pets?

The queen has always loved animals. Her father, George VI, started a family tradition of keeping corgis as pets and the queen is happy to keep it going.

When did Elizabeth marry?

During the war, Princess Elizabeth had fallen in love with the dashing Prince Philip of Greece, a third cousin who was serving in the Royal Navy. Her parents were not so sure that her young romance would provide her with a suitable husband. But Queen Mary, the princess's grandmother, knew that Elizabeth was serious and she considered Prince Philip a good addition to the royal family. So Princess Elizabeth married Philip Mountbatten, Duke of Edinburgh, on November 20, 1947. Today, they have three sons, one daughter and six grandchildren.

THE FUTURE RULER?

When it comes to choosing the next ruler of Britain, the boys in the family are always chosen before the girls. That means the eldest prince in the family follows his mother or father to the throne. If there are no boys, then the girls might become queens, chosen according to age. If there are no children to inherit the throne, the brother of the king might rule in his place. At the moment, Prince Charles is heir to the crown.

Crime and Punishment

Where does the word 'crime' come from?

The word 'crime' comes from Latin, the language of the Romans, who conquered much of Britain almost 2,000 years ago. They were the first people to have law courts, trials and written laws.

Did the Romans have different laws for different people?

In Roman Britain, people belonged to different social groups, and each group had different rights. At the top, with the most rights, were the Roman citizens. Below them, were free non-citizens. At the bottom were slaves, people owned by other people, and they had no rights at all. Punishments were much harsher for slaves and non-citizens than for citizens.

Why were thieves cursed?

When people were robbed, they often asked the gods to punish the thief. They wrote curses on little sheets of lead and offered them to the gods, burying them or throwing them into holy springs. A typical curse from Bath says: 'Docimedis has lost two gloves. He asks that the person who stole them lose his mind and his eyes in the temple'.

Where were criminals executed?

Executions took place in large open-air buildings called amphitheatres. The Romans had very bloodthirsty tastes, and huge crowds flocked to amphitheatres to watch people die. So far, nineteen Roman amphitheatres have been found in Britain.

A woman asks the gods to punish a criminal.

Why was it a crime to be a Christian?

In the second century AD, a new religion, Christianity, spread throughout the Roman empire. The Romans feared that their gods would become angry and punish the whole empire for the Christians' behaviour. So they made Christianity a crime.

Gladiators battle it out in the amphitheatre.

GLADIATORS

Gladiators were professional fighters who would fight other gladiators and wild beasts in the amphitheatres. They had to be ready to fight to the death. Becoming a gladiator was another punishment given to criminals and to slaves who upset their owners.

Who was the first Christian known to be executed in Britain?

A Roman soldier called Alban was beheaded for the crime of being a Christian in the third or fourth century AD. The town where he was killed, Verulamium, was later renamed St Albans in his honour.

How were crimes punished by the Romans?

For minor crimes, such as not paying debts, citizens were stripped of their citizenship. Non-citizens were often condemned to slavery and may have been forced to work as oarsmen, rowing warships, or as miners. For serious crimes, the punishment was execution.

When did it become a crime not to be a Christian?

In the year AD 312, a Christian, called Constantine, became Roman Emperor. He made Christianity the official religion of the empire, and set about converting everybody to his religion. Soon it was against the law to worship the old Roman gods.

What was blood money?

Blood money, or wergild, was a fine. It was paid by someone who had committed a crime to the victim. The idea behind blood money was to stop families from feuding.

How much did people pay for blood money?

Every crime had a price. The oldest Anglo-Saxon laws list the prices which had to be paid for various injuries, right down to a bruise and a lost thumbnail.

A sheriff sits and listens to two sides of an argument.

What was a blood feud?

In the fifth century, much of Britain had been settled by the Anglo-Saxons, or English, who crossed the sea from northern Europe. They believed that if a man was murdered, his relatives had to get revenge. This meant that a murder was avenged with another murder, which had to be avenged in turn. These could develop into deadly quarrels between families, called blood feuds, which could last for many years.

Who was responsible for law and order?

By the tenth century, England was divided into areas called shires. Each shire had a royal official, called a shire-reeve, or sheriff, who was responsible for the law. There was also a shire court, where people were tried for crimes and where quarrels were sorted out.

What happened at a trial?

The accused would try to get people who knew him, called 'oath helpers', to swear that he was innocent. The accuser would also have his own oath helpers to swear to the guilt of the accused. The outcome depended on who had the most important oath helpers.

A man is tried by hot iron ordeal.

What was the hot iron ordeal?

The accused had to carry a heated iron down the middle of the church. His hand was then bandaged. If it had healed after three days, he was declared innocent. An unhealed or infected wound was considered a sign of guilt.

What was trial by ordeal?

If a decision could not be reached by oaths, the accused had to go through a 'trial by ordeal'. An ordeal was a test which took place in a church. It was believed that the result of the test would be a sign from God, showing the guilt or innocence of the accused.

What was the cold water ordeal?

The accused was tied up in a crouching position, with his wrists behind his knees. He was then lowered into water using a rope with a knot tied in it at a point matching the length of his hair. If he sank down to the knot, he was said to be innocent. Guilty people floated.

How did the Anglo-Saxons execute criminals?

Criminals were hanged by the neck from a tree or a wooden frame called a gallows. The advantage of hanging was that the killing took place up in the air, where it could be seen by a large crowd and everyone could witness that justice had been done. Hanging became the main method of execution in Britain right up until the 1960s.

WERGILD

If you had money, you could often be let off crimes by paying the wergild. However, criminals who kept offending, or who could not pay, were harshly punished. They might have a hand or foot cut off or they could be executed.

Who were the robbers from the sea?

From 787, the coast of Britain was attacked by fierce raiders from Norway and Denmark, called Vikings. To begin with the Vikings came as robbers, taking the gold from English monasteries, and kidnapping the monks who lived there to use as slaves. Later in the 840s, Viking armies arrived to conquer and settle.

Did the Vikings have laws?

The very word 'law' comes from the Vikings. The Vikings had many laws, which were memorised by men called 'lawspeakers', and passed down from one generation to another. Eventually, when the Vikings became Christian, some of their laws were written down by monks.

Where did the Vikings try wrongdoers?

Vikings held regular open-air law meetings, where new laws were made and criminals were tried and punished. These meetings were called 'Things'.

THE DANELAW

The area of England where Vikings from Denmark settled became known as 'The Danelaw', because Danish laws were in force there. It included East Anglia, Lincolnshire and Yorkshire.

Where were Viking Things held?

Thanks to place names, we know where some Viking Things took place. These include Tingwall (Orkney), Law Ting Holm (Shetland), Tynwald (Isle of Man), Dingwall (Highland, Scotland) and Thingwall (Merseyside).

Why did the Vikings attack monasteries?

Monasteries were the homes of holy men called monks who spent their lives in work and prayer. Monks did not know how to fight, so they were easy to rob and kidnap. Monasteries were also full of treasures, such as jewelled crosses and books decorated with silver and gold.

A monk pleads for his life as his church is raided by Viking warriors.

How were decisions made at Things?

There was often a vote. Viking men would show if they agreed to a decision by waving their swords, spears and battleaxes in the air. In the region of Danelaw, law meetings were known as 'wapentakes', which means 'weapon taking'.

What happened to outlaws?

They usually had to flee their homes and try to find somewhere else to live. Many sailed off to other lands which had been settled by Vikings, such as Iceland and Ireland. Others went back to the old Viking way of life and became sea raiders again.

What was Danegeld?

In the 980s, there was a new wave of Viking raids in England. This time, the raiders offered to go away in peace if they were paid money. The payment, was called 'Danegeld' – Dane gold; in fact, it was usually paid not in gold, but in silver.

How were criminals punished?

A typical Viking punishment was to be declared an outlaw. An outlaw was someone who was 'outside the law' and no longer had any rights. Anybody could kill an outlaw without being punished.

How much Danegeld was paid?

Each year the Vikings came back, they demanded more Danegeld than the year before. In the year 991, the English paid 4,500 kg of silver. By 1012, the amount had risen to 8,200 kg.

Why did the Danegeld payments end?

Cnut, the Viking ruler who had been leading the raids for Danegeld, decided to stay in England and make himself king. The English were too weak to resist him and, in 1016, he was crowned ruler.

Danegeld is brought to the Vikings.

A hunter tries to hide the deer that
he shot and killed.

Why was it a crime to kill a deer?

In 1066, England was conquered by the Normans, led by
William I. William loved hunting wild animals, such as deer and
boar, and after he became King, he made it a crime for ordinary
people to hunt these animals. An English writer said that
William loved the deer as if they were his own children.

Why did French become the language of law?

The Normans spoke French, so that became the language spoken in law courts.
Even today many legal words we use are French. They include judge, jury, court,
assize, trial, verdict and legal.

REGARDERS, FORESTERS AND VERDERERS

Forest laws were enforced by an army of royal officials. They included
regarders (inspectors), foresters and verderers. The verderers had the
special job of protecting the greenwood.

What was forest law?

William the Conqueror declared that
much of the country was 'forest',
meaning land set aside for the king to
hunt in. It included villages and open
areas as well as woodland. Later
kings increased the forests until, by
the thirteenth century, they covered a
third of the whole kingdom. Wild
animals, such as red deer and boar,
were protected by 'forest laws'.

What were crimes against forest law?

The worst crime was poaching, or illegal hunting. Poaching comes from the French word 'pocher', meaning to pocket. Another crime was damaging the 'vert' (greenwood), the growing trees and undergrowth where the deer and boar sheltered.

How were poachers tried and punished?

Every seven years, cases were heard by a travelling royal court. An accused person might have to spend years waiting in prison to be tried. Those found guilty of poaching could be blinded or have a hand cut off.

Who was Robin Hood?

By the 1300s, people were telling stories of an outlaw, called Robin Hood, whose hiding place was the royal forest in either Nottinghamshire or Yorkshire. He lived in the greenwood with a group of men, hunting deer with his bow and arrow. Simply living like this was a crime, but Robin also robbed from the rich to give to the poor.

Was Robin Hood a real person?

Nobody knows if there was ever a real Robin Hood. But the stories about him show how much people hated the forest laws. Hundreds of English places are named after the outlaw. They include Robin Hood's Barrow (Dorset); Robin Hood's Leap (Derbyshire); and Robin Hood's Bay (Yorkshire).

What was trial by combat?

The Normans introduced a new type of ordeal, called trial by combat. People accused of crimes could fight their accuser to prove their innocence. In some cases, such as arguments over land, they could use a 'champion', a skilled knight who would fight on their behalf. But a man accused of murder had to fight in person.

What happened to the loser in a trial by combat?

The Normans thought that God would not allow an innocent man to be beaten. So if a man accused of murder lost his fight, he was judged guilty and hanged.

A loser in a trial by combat who now faces hanging.

What was ducking a scold?

A woman who shouted at her husband or neighbours was called a scold, and scolding was against the law. As a punishment scolds were often ducked in ponds and rivers. They were tied to a seat on the end of a plank overhanging the water and ducked, while everybody made fun of them.

A woman sits in a ducking chair.

What was a shaming punishment?

From Norman times until the 1700s, many punishments were used to make wrongdoers feel ashamed. Shaming punishments included being made to sit backwards on a horse and paraded through the streets; being locked in a wooden frame, called the stocks, and pelted with rubbish; and being ducked in a pond or river.

What was the point of a shaming punishment?

The aim was to make the offender look foolish. This was a powerful punishment at a time when most people lived in small towns and villages. Everyone knew everybody else's business, and they worried about what their neighbours thought of them.

Why were only women called scolds?

Women were expected to live quietly and obey their husbands. A woman who shouted in the street was seen as a public nuisance. But people also looked down on husbands who could not control their wives.

What was a church court?

From the mid-1100s, the Church was given the right to hold its own courts where people were tried for various offences. Any sort of bad behaviour thought to upset God, was called a sin, and could be punished by a church court. Church courts also dealt with the crimes of clerics (monks, priests and nuns).

A scold's bridle.

What sorts of bad behaviour did church courts punish?

People were tried for all sorts of offences, including drunkenness, fighting during a church service and throwing stones at a church. You could also be tried if you were caught dancing or playing football on a Sunday as this was supposed to be a holy day.

What was benefit of clergy?

Clerics had the right to be tried in the church courts which could not sentence people to death. Many criminals facing a death sentence, for crimes such as murder, claimed to be clerics. To prove they were clerics, they had to say a verse from the Bible. This was nicknamed the 'neck verse', because it saved their necks from hanging.

THE SCOLD'S BRIDLE

The scold's bridle, or branks, was an uncomfortable punishment used in Scotland. The scold was made to wear a metal cage over her head with a bar which stuck into her mouth, and stopped her from speaking.

Why were people branded on the thumb?

Criminals who claimed benefit of clergy were branded on the thumb with a red-hot iron bar. This was so that, if they were tried again, the courts would know by the scar that they were clerics.

How did church courts punish people?

Church courts made people do public penances acts to show everybody that the offenders were sorry. As a typical penance, offenders had to stand up in church, wearing a white sheet and holding a sign describing their bad behaviour.

This man is riding a horse backwards as a shaming punishment.

How was treason punished?

The punishment for treason was to be 'hanged, drawn and quartered'. The traitor was dragged behind a horse to the place of execution. Then he was hanged, but taken down while still alive. He was then 'drawn' – his stomach was cut open and his insides were pulled out and burned in front of him. His head was then cut off, and his body was chopped into four parts – quarters.

What is treason?

Treason is a crime against your ruler or your country. Since the Middle Ages, many people have been tried for plotting to kill the king or queen, or for helping foreign enemies during a war. Such people were called traitors.

A criminal is dragged to his execution.

Why were traitors chopped into quarters?

This was so that their bodies could be displayed in different parts of the country. The idea was to show as many people as possible the terrible punishment for treason.

Which famous Scottish hero was quartered?

Sir William Wallace was a Scot who fought against English rule. To the English king, Edward I, Wallace was a traitor. After he was executed in 1305, his quarters were displayed at Newcastle, Berwick, Stirling and Perth and his head was stuck on a spike on London Bridge.

Were traitors always hanged, drawn and quartered?

Noblemen and noblewomen were usually allowed a quicker death, by beheading, often at the Tower of London. One entrance to the Tower is still called the 'Traitors' Gate'.

What was the Gunpowder Plot?

In 1605, a group of English Catholics plotted to blow up the Houses of Parliament and kill the king, James I. They wanted to replace James, who was a Protestant, with a Catholic. But they were discovered, and the man sent to light the fuse, Guy Fawkes, was caught in the act.

How many queens have been beheaded?

King Henry VIII executed two of his wives, Anne Boleyn in 1536, and Catherine Howard in 1542. In 1587, Henry's daughter, Queen Elizabeth I, had her cousin, Mary Queen of Scots, beheaded for plotting against her.

Can a king be tried for treason?

In the 1640s, there was a war between the king, Charles I, and the English Parliament. Charles lost, and was put on trial for starting a war against his own people. He was found guilty of treason and, in 1649, he was executed.

The Gunpowder Plotters are discovered.

What was a cutpurse?

In Tudor times (1485-1603), people carried their money in purses, which they hung from strings attached to their belts. Cutpurses were thieves who would cut the strings to steal the purses.

SOMETHING FISHY

An angler was a thief who robbed houses and shops by lifting goods through open windows. It was called 'angling' (fishing) because the thief used a long pole with a hook on the end, like a fishing rod.

What is a professional criminal?

Professional criminals are people who live solely by crime. The first real professional criminals appeared in Tudor times. Each criminal tended to stick to one type of crime, such as cutting purses or stealing horses.

What was canting?

Tudor criminals had their own secret language, called 'canting'. This allowed them to speak to each other without letting outsiders know what they were talking about. Each type of criminal had his own nickname. A horse thief was called a 'prigger of prances'. Sheep-stealing was called the 'bleating rig', and 'nipping a bung' meant cutting a purse.

What was a 'counterfeit crank'?

It was against the law for healthy people to beg. The punishment was to be tied behind a cart and whipped out of town. 'Counterfeit cranks' were healthy beggars who got around the law by pretending to be sick or disabled. They might wear bandages or walk with crutches. 'Abram men' were beggars who faked madness, and 'dommerers' pretended that they could not speak.

What was a bellman?

A bellman was an official who patrolled the dark streets of towns at night, watching out for crimes and fires. Every hour, he would ring his bell and cry out the time.

A bellman patrols the streets.

Where did cutpurses learn to steal?

In 1585, a man called Wotton was arrested for running a school for cutpurses. He taught young boys to lift coins from a purse with bells sewn onto it. Boys practised until they could remove the coins without ringing the bells.

What was a House of Correction?

In 1556, the government came up with a new punishment for begging. It was to be locked up in a special prison, called a 'House of Correction', and forced to work. Grown-ups might chop firewood, while children often learned a trade, such as shoemaking. The first was opened in London, at Bridewell Palace. By the 1600s, there were 'Bridewells', as they were called, all over the country.

What was new about Bridewells?

Earlier prisons, called gaols, were simply places to hold people awaiting trial or punishment. Now prison itself began to be seen as a punishment. Houses of Correction were also supposed to 'correct' criminals – teach them to live better lives. This was the beginning of the prison system we have today.

A man in a pillory is ridiculed by the public.

Why was witchcraft a crime?

Witchcraft is the use of magic spells
to cause harm. Belief in witchcraft
goes back thousands of years, but it
was only in the 1500s that people
began to see witches as a threat to
society. In 1542, witchcraft was made
a crime punishable by hanging.

What was a witchfinder?

A man or woman who claimed to be able to hunt down witches
was called a witchfinder. The most famous was Matthew
Hopkins, who called himself the
'Witchfinder General'. In the 1640s, he
accused 180 women and 30 men of
being witches. Almost a hundred of
them were hanged.

The witchfinder asks the public
for help in finding witches.

Why did people believe in witches?

In the 1500s, the true causes of most
diseases were not understood. When
people suddenly fell ill or when their
farm animals died, they looked
around for someone or something to
blame. Often, they blamed their
troubles on spells cast by their
neighbours.

What sort of people were accused of being witches?

People who did not get on with their
neighbours were often accused of
being witches, especially if they lived
alone and had no-one to defend them.
Most people accused of witchcraft
were old women, but men and even
children were also accused.

What was a witch's familiar?

Witches were thought to have
'familiars' – evil spirit helpers which
took the shape of animals, such as
cats or toads. The witches were
supposed to feed their familiars on
their own blood.

What was a 'witch's mark'?

Witches were thought to have special marks on their body, left by the devil or by their familiars. So witchfinders would search a person's skin for any unusual spots or moles. In Scotland, people believed that a witch's mark would not bleed if you pricked it.

Why were witches watched?

Another way to catch a witch was to make her sit on a stool and watch her to see if her familiar came into the room to be fed. The watchers kept the witch awake, often for days on end. If the witch started to fall asleep, he or she was forced to stand up and walk around the room. Many became so desperate for sleep that they confessed to being witches.

Who were the last British people to be hanged as witches?

The last witchcraft hanging took place in Exeter in 1682. Three women, Temperance Lloyd, Susannah Edwards and Mary Trembles, were hanged for using spells to make their neighbours fall ill.

THE END OF WITCHCRAFT TRIALS

By the late 1600s, most educated people had come to doubt whether witchcraft really existed. Although cases were still brought, the courts usually found the accused innocent. In 1735, the law against witchcraft was dropped.

What was 'swimming' a witch?

Another strange idea about witches was that they would not sink in water. The suspect was tied up and lowered into a pond. If the accused floated, he or she was said to be guilty. If the accused sank he or she had been proved innocent and was quickly dragged out again.

Swimming a witch.

What is piracy?

Piracy means robbery at sea. There have been pirates ever since Roman times, but the most famous pirates lived between 1650 and 1720. This was the 'Golden Age of Piracy', when British pirates sailed the Caribbean Sea and the Atlantic Ocean.

Blackbeard was one of the most fearsome pirates.

Who was the most frightening pirate?

Edward Teach, nicknamed 'Blackbeard', made himself look as terrifying as possible. His face was hidden behind a massive black beard, which he twisted with ribbons. When he went into battle, he stuck burning lengths of cord under his hat to make himself look even more frightening.

How successful was Blackbeard?

Between 1713 and 1718, Blackbeard captured more than 45 ships. But he was eventually hunted down by the British Navy. On November 22, 1718, he was killed during a bloody battle and the sailors chopped off his head and hung it from the front of their ship.

What was a cutlass?

The pirate's favourite weapon was a short sword, called a cutlass. It was perfect for fighting in small spaces such as on the deck of a ship.

Why did pirates fly a 'jolly roger'?

When pirates went into battle, they would often fly a black flag, nicknamed a 'jolly roger'. It was decorated with various pictures to do with death or fighting, such as a skull and cross-bones, a skeleton or a crossed pair of cutlasses. By flying the jolly roger, the pirates hoped to scare their victims into giving up without a fight.

PIRATES BY APPOINTMENT

A privateer was a pirate who only attacked ships belonging to the enemies of his country. Privateers were given special permission by the king or queen to attack enemy ships and ports.

Were women ever pirates?

Mary Read and Anne Bonney were pirates who dressed as men and served on the same ship, under Captain 'Calico Jack' Rackham. In 1721, when they were captured by the Navy, Mary and Anne fought more fiercely than any of the men on board.

Anne Bonney and Mary Read.

Who was the most successful privateer?

In 1671, a Welsh privateer called Henry Morgan led a daring attack on Panama, one of the richest Spanish ports in the Americas. Leading a fleet of 36 ships and over 1,800 men, Morgan captured Panama, and burned it to the ground. He carried away a fortune in gold, silver, jewels and slaves. Morgan was later given a knighthood and made the governor of Jamaica.

What happened to Mary Read and Anne Bonney?

Anne Bonney and Mary Read were sentenced to hang, but they were let off because they were expecting babies. Mary died of sickness in prison, but Anne's fate is not known. She was allowed to see Calico Jack one last time, on the night before his execution. She told him, 'I am sorry to see you here, but if you had fought like a man, you need not have been hanged like a dog.'

What is smuggling?

Smuggling is the illegal movement of goods from one country to another. There are two reasons to smuggle: either to avoid paying duty (taxes); or because it is against the law to buy and sell the goods in the first place.

What goods were smuggled into Britain?

Brandy, wine, tea, tobacco and coffee were all smuggled to Britain from France. These goods were all smuggled in to avoid paying duties. In Britain, half of all the tea drunk and tobacco smoked was said to be smuggled.

Where did smuggling take place?

In the eighteenth century, smuggling was common all around the British coast, but especially in Western Scotland, Cornwall, Kent and Sussex. These were ideal smuggling bases. The Cornish and Scottish coasts are full of little inlets and caves, where smugglers could land without being seen and hide their cargoes. Kent and Sussex are the closest parts of Britain to France, so smugglers did not have far to sail.

What were 'owlers'?

'Owlers' was the nickname of Kent and Sussex wool smugglers. It is not known how they got this name. It may come from 'wooller', or it may be because they worked at night, like owls.

Why was wool smuggled?

It was against the law to sell English wool abroad – only woven cloth could be sold. This law was passed to help English weavers sell their goods. Yet sheep farmers could get better prices for their wool in France than by selling it to the English weavers, so they started smuggling wool across the Channel.

A coastguard scans the coast for smugglers.

PUT THAT LIGHT OUT!

In 1619, a lighthouse was being built on the Lizard headland in Cornwall. The locals attacked the builders and pulled the half-built lighthouse down. They did not want a lighthouse that would stop ships being wrecked on their coast.

Which was the most famous smuggling gang?

The most feared smugglers were the Hawkhurst Gang, named after the Kent village where they were based. They could call on 500 mounted armed men and 500 packhorses to carry their goods. The gang's career lasted from 1735 until 1748, when their leader, Arthur Gray, was hanged for murdering a customs officer.

Dragoons clash with smugglers who have been caught red-handed.

How did the government try to stop smuggling?

Customs officers patrolled the coasts in small ships, called cutters. On land, soldiers called dragoons tried to hunt down the smugglers. But the forces of law and order were often outnumbered by large and well-armed gangs.

What did people think of smugglers?

Most ordinary people did not see smuggling as a crime. They saw smugglers as people who sold luxury goods, such as brandy, cheaply.

What were wreckers?

People living in Cornwall and the Scilly Islands made an extra living by stealing the cargoes of wrecked and stranded ships.

Did wreckers cause wrecks?

Many stories were told of Cornish wreckers luring ships to their doom, by shining lamps from rocks, making the sailors think that a harbour was nearby.

Who were the gentlemen of the road?

'Gentlemen of the road' was a nickname given to highwaymen – thieves who robbed travellers on Britain's roads. The most famous and successful highwaymen lived between 1645 and 1750. At the time, travel by road was increasing, but there was no police force to protect travellers. There were also new reliable firearms, which meant that a single highwayman could easily hold up a coach and rob its passengers.

Were highwaymen really gentlemen?

Highwaymen were called gentlemen because they were good horsemen. At the time, it was rare for people from poor backgrounds to own a decent horse, or to know how to ride one.

What was a 'thief-taker'?

'Thief-takers' were people who hunted down criminals, such as highwaymen, and handed them over to be tried, in return for a reward.

Who was the first criminal mastermind?

Jonathan Wild was a thief-taker who was also a master criminal. His speciality was returning stolen goods to their owners for a reward. What the owners did not know was that Wild had been behind the robberies in the first place.

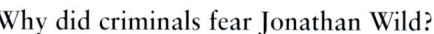

Why did criminals fear Jonathan Wild?

London criminals obeyed Wild because they feared that he would hand them over to the law. In his role as thief-taker, he had more than 60 criminals hanged – mostly men who had double-crossed him. Wild's crimes were eventually discovered and, in 1725, he went to the gallows.

A highwayman prepares to stop a coach and horses.

Grave robbers work under the cover of darkness.

What was grave robbing?

Grave robbing was digging up dead bodies from graveyards and selling them to surgeons. Grave robbers were also known as body-snatchers or 'sack-em-up men', because they carried the bodies away in sacks.

WHY DID THE SURGEONS WANT DEAD BODIES?

Surgeons needed bodies to cut up in order to teach their students medicine. They would pay good money for a fresh body, and they would ask no questions about where it had come from.

Who escaped from prison five times?

Jack Shepherd was a burglar who was famous for escaping from one prison after another. In 1724, he was locked up in the strongest cell in Newgate Prison, weighed down with heavy chains which were fixed to the floor. Despite this, Jack managed to pick his locks with a bent nail and climb up a chimney into another cell. He then broke through six bolted doors, each one stronger than the last, and got away.

What happened to Shepherd after his escape?

Jack Shepherd was so proud of his escape that he celebrated by having a party in a neighbouring gin-shop. The news spread, and Jack was soon recaptured. To stop him escaping again, he was constantly watched and a month after his famous escape, Jack was hanged.

What was Tyburn Tree?

Tyburn Tree was the nickname given to London's three-legged gallows, where men, women and children were executed from 1196 until 1783.

How often were people hanged at Tyburn?

Hangings took place eight to ten times a year, on certain Mondays. These 'hanging Mondays' were public holidays, and huge crowds went to Tyburn to watch the criminals die.

Why did the gallows have three legs?

This allowed the hangman to execute more people. Eight could be hanged from each cross-beam, so 24 could be killed at one time.

How did the criminals get to Tyburn?

Condemned criminals were taken from Newgate Prison, in the city of London, five kilometres west to Tyburn. They travelled by cart, often sitting on their own coffins.

HANGING DAYS AND HOLIDAYS

The government wanted as many people as possible to see executions, so the days on which criminals were hanged were made into holidays. The idea was to teach people to obey the law and to learn that crime did not pay.

What did the crowd think of the criminals going to Tyburn?

Criminals like Jack Shepherd were seen as heroes, particularly if they went bravely to their deaths. The crowd cheered them, gave them bunches of flowers and raised their hats to salute them.

A condemned man enjoys his last drink on the journey to the gallows.

What sort of crimes could you be hanged for?

In the 1720s, there were more than 200 crimes punishable by hanging. They included smuggling wool, using a disguise while committing a crime, damaging Westminster Bridge and sending threatening letters.

What happened to the bodies after they were dead?

People rushed forward to touch them, for the body of a hanged person was thought to have the power to cure illnesses.

What was a gibbet?

From 1752 until 1834, people who were hanged for certain crimes, such as piracy and murder, had their bodies displayed in gibbets, which were metal cages, hanging from posts.

A pirate's body hangs from the gibbet as a warning to others not to take to a life of crime.

Why did hangings at Tyburn end?

As London grew, the West End, where Tyburn was, became a fashionable area and rich people did not want to have hangings, with rowdy crowds, on their doorsteps. In 1783, the execution site was moved to the street in front of Newgate Prison.

CRACKSMEN AND SNAKESMEN

Victorian burglars were nicknamed 'cracksmen'. They sometimes used small boys, called 'snakesmen', to help them break into houses. The boys got in by wriggling through narrow windows.

Why did the first policemen wear top hats?

It was hoped that people would look up to policemen if they wore top hats. Top hats were worn by gentlemen, so they were a sign of respectability. They also made policemen look taller and easier to spot. Unfortunately, a top hat was a perfect target for stone throwers and by the 1860s, top hats had been replaced by helmets.

Who were the 'peelers'?

As the number of criminals rose, the old ways of keeping law and order were no longer good enough. In 1829, Sir Robert Peel set up the first proper police force in London. The policemen were nicknamed 'peelers' and 'bobbies' after Sir Robert Peel. Soon, there were police forces all over the country.

A policeman catches children throwing stones at him.

What were snoozers, snow-gatherers and bug hunters?

In the Victorian period (1837-1901), several new types of professional criminal appeared. Just like Tudor criminals, these Victorians had their own nicknames. 'Snoozers' were well-dressed men who booked themselves into hotels and then robbed all the guests' rooms while they were sleeping. 'Snow-gatherers' stole clothes which had been left to dry on hedges and washing-lines. 'Bug-hunters' were thieves who waited outside pubs at night to rob the drunks.

What was garotting?

Garotting was a type of street robbery which appeared in the 1850s. Garotters usually worked in threes. Two would grab a victim from behind, one of them gripping him around the throat and half-strangling him. The third would then go through his pockets. The whole robbery would be over in less than a minute, leaving the surprised victim lying, out of breath, on the pavement.

Garotters attack a wealthy gentleman and pick his pocket.

Why did the number of criminals rise?

In the nineteenth century, the population of Britain more than tripled, from 10.5 million in 1801, to 37 million in 1901. People moved from the countryside to new towns and cities, which grew at an amazing rate. These cities had terrible slum areas, where many people turned to crime in order to live. In the first half of the century, the number of people found guilty of crimes each year rose from around 2,700 to over 20,000. By 1851, there were more than 13,000 criminals in London alone.

What did the police do?

Policemen walked the streets, armed with a truncheon, keeping an eye out for trouble. Their main aim was to stop crimes happening. People were less likely to break the law if they saw a policeman walking by.

Did the public like the police?

The middle and upper classes welcomed the police. But most poor people thought that they were only there to protect the rich. They gave them nasty nicknames, such as 'crushers', 'blue locusts' and 'blue drones'. According to one Victorian newspaper, people in poor areas looked on policemen as an enemy 'whom it is right to kick and beat whenever that can be done with safety'.

Prisoners exercise in the prison yard at Pentonville.

When could Victorian prisoners meet each other?

The only time prisoners in Pentonville saw other prisoners was when they were taken into a yard to exercise. They had to wear masks while they exercised, walking round in a circle.

Why did the Victorians have to build new prisons?

In the early 1800s, the number of crimes carrying the death penalty was cut down until, by 1841, only murderers were likely to be hanged. At the same time, far more people were being found guilty of crimes. The old prisons, such as Newgate, could not cope with all the convicts, so the Victorians began a huge prison-building programme.

Why were British prisoners sent to Australia?

Another answer to the prison shortage was to ship people abroad. Between 1787 and 1868, 160,000 men, women and children were transported (sent by ship) to Australia. At the time, Australia was being settled by British people. The convicts were sent there as a punishment, and to provide free labour for the settlers. The voyage took six months, and the convicts had to spend much of their time locked in cages, below deck.

Why did transportation end?

Thanks to the new prisons, by 1868 it was cheaper to imprison convicts than to ship them halfway around the world. The Australians had started complaining about having the worst British people sent to them. The discovery of gold in Australia also meant that poor people now wanted to go there, so transportation was no longer seen as a punishment.

What were the new prisons like?

The new Victorian prisons, such as Pentonville, were designed to make criminals reform, or turn away from crime. To stop them being a bad influence on each other, convicts were kept apart from each other at all times. They spent most of their days alone in a cell. This was called the 'separate system'.

Why did the prisoners have to wear masks?

Masks stopped the prisoners from recognising each other and from making friends. For the same reason, they were never called by their names. Every prisoner was given a number, which they had to answer to as if it was their name.

A prison hulk.

FLOATING PRISONS

One short-term answer to the prison shortage was to use old warships, called hulks. These were anchored near naval bases, such as Woolwich and Portsmouth. During the day, the prisoners came ashore and worked, breaking rocks or unloading coal, and at night they returned to the ship. To stop them jumping over the side and swimming to freedom, they had to wear heavy iron chains. Hulks stopped being used in 1858, when enough new prisons had been built.

What was picking oakum?

Picking oakum was a type of work done by prisoners. Oakum was the nickname of a tarred length of old rope from ships. Prisoners had to unpick the oakum so that it could be made into new rope, or used to caulk the sides of ships (plug the gaps between the planks).

What was the silent system?

Under the silent system, prisoners picked oakum in large rooms, sitting side by side with their fellow prisoners. They were not allowed to talk to each other. Like the separate system, this was to stop prisoners from being a bad influence on each other. This system was used in the old prisons, where there were not enough cells to keep everyone apart.

What was 'grinding the wind'?

Another prison punishment was the treadmill, a great wheel with steps, which the convicts turned by climbing. It was like the wheel of a mill, except that it served no practical purpose, such as grinding wheat. So it was called 'grinding the wind'.

A prisoner carries out his cranking punishment.

What was turning a crank?

A crank was a metal drum with a handle, that was filled with sand. A convict had to turn the crank as a punishment. He would not get any food until he had turned the crank a set number of times. A dial showed the number of times the handle had been turned, so the prisoner could be left alone while he was punished.

Why did the Victorians stop hanging people in public?

The behaviour of the crowds who came to watch hangings showed that they did not put people off crime. Far from learning to respect the law, many people seemed to be on the side of the criminals, so from 1868, murderers were hanged inside prisons.

Explorers and Adventurers

Who thought the world was flat?

Although ancient Greek mathematicians had worked out that the world was round, the Christian Church produced maps in medieval times showing the world as a flat disc surrounded by water. At its centre was the holy city of Jerusalem. Early explorers sailed towards the horizon terrified that if they went too far, they might topple over the edge.

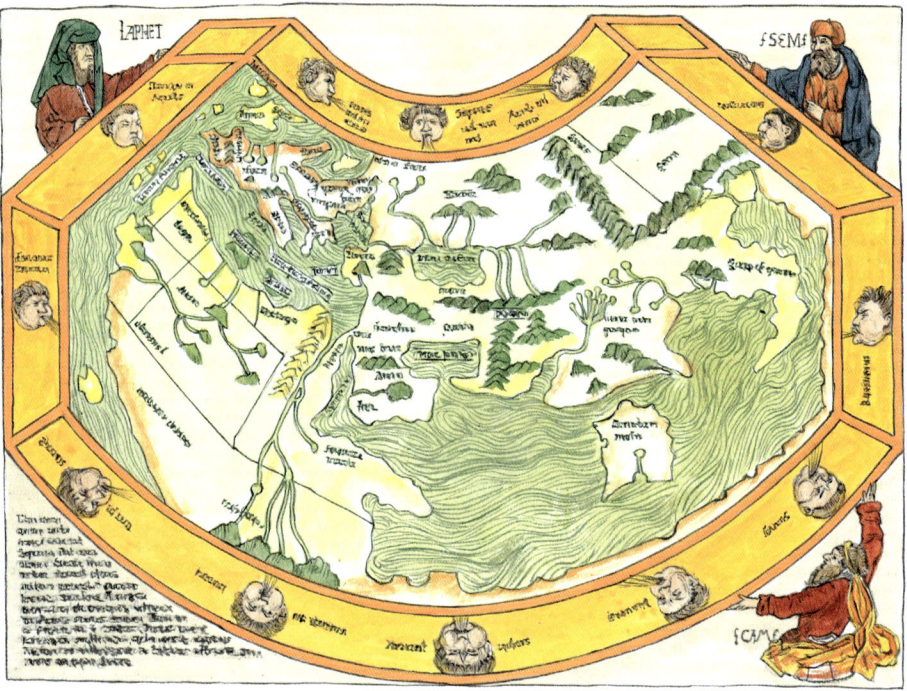

What did explorers do with goat skin?

The maps carried by explorers on the early voyages of discovery were often drawn on the skin of a goat. They were known as 'portolan' charts.

MARCO POLO

The Italian explorer Marco Polo wrote the greatest travel book of medieval times, after spending 24 years from 1271 to 1295 exploring Asia. People in Europe could hardly believe his amazing tales of paper money, coal, tigers and crocodiles, jewels as big as apples, cities with 12,000 bridges and palaces where 6,000 people could dine.

How many continents did people think there were?

In medieval times, people thought there were just three enormous continents, Europe, Asia and Africa, and perhaps a mysterious and enormous southern continent. They believed that most of the globe was land, with a small amount of water. In fact, more than two-thirds of the globe is covered by water!

Who thought they would be boiled alive?

In medieval times, explorers were afraid that when they reached the Equator, the heat from the sun would be so great that the sea would boil, their ships would catch fire and the sailors would be burnt to a cinder.

A medieval map based on the maps of the ancient Greek astronomer Ptolemy.

Were early maps accurate?

No, early maps were often based on myths and mistakes. A famous map was produced by the Greek astronomer and thinker Ptolemy. He calculated the earth's circumference to be about 29,000 kilometres, which was about 11,000 kilometres too small!

Who first sailed around the British Isles?

The ancient Greek explorer Pytheas sailed from France in the fourth century BC to look for the western edge of the world. But instead of the world's end, he discovered Land's End on the western tip of Britain. Pytheas then sailed right around Britain, discovering the Orkneys on the way.

Were there monsters living in distant lands?

Early explorers expected to discover monsters in distant lands, because travellers such as the Italian Marco Polo heard many tales of such creatures during their adventures. Sea serpents were drawn on maps made in the sixteenth century and geography books showed a world full of giants, dwarves, unicorns and sphinxes. There were also stories about strange races of people with heads like wolves, or with giant feet that they used as umbrellas!

Who discovered the 'Promised Land'?

St Brendan was a monk living in Ireland in the sixth century, who sailed north-west in a tiny skin boat called a curragh. He discovered a 'Promised Land', which might have been the Hebrides, Iceland or even America.

A map showing some of the myths and monsters of the medieval world.

What was the Northwest Passage?

Martin Frobisher on Baffin Island, with a rock that he believed to be gold.

By the sixteenth century, European traders were desperate to fill their ships' holds with the precious silks, spices and jewels of the 'Indies' (India, Japan, China and South-East Asia). But the only sea routes to the Indies were long and dangerous voyages to the south. Some people believed there was an easier route, across the top of the world between the north coast of America and the ice of the Arctic. For the next four centuries, explorers and adventurers set sail in search of this elusive 'Northwest Passage'.

Who thought he had struck gold?

In 1576, Yorkshireman Martin Frobisher discovered some shiny rocks on Baffin Island off the coast of Canada, while searching for the Northwest Passage in his ship *Gabriel*. He made two more voyages to the island, and sailed home with thousands of these rocks. But they turned out to be worthless, and his 'fool's gold' was used to repair English roads.

Why did a man bite his tongue in half?

Frobisher also captured an Inuit man, who was so angry he bit his own tongue in half! Back in England, the queen granted the tongueless Inuit permission to hunt for birds, and he was often seen shooting swans and ducks from his canoe on the River Thames!

Why did John Davis dance a hornpipe?

Davis was an English navigator who made three Arctic voyages in search of the famous Passage from 1585 to 1587. His sailors kept the local Inuit people friendly by dancing a hornpipe for them, playing football and taking part in wrestling matches.

Did Davis find the Passage?

No, but he did discover Davis Strait, which offered an entrance to the Northwest Passage. Unfortunately, Davis had to turn back when his ship was halted by gales and nearly crushed by enormous icebergs.

Did Henry see a mermaid?

Hudson recorded in his diary that one of his crew looked over the side of the ship and saw a mermaid with a woman's body and a tail like that of a porpoise. However, it was probably a seal or walrus, but who knows?

MISLEADING MAP

Martin Frobisher followed a map drawn by an Italian called Nicolò Zeno, which showed lands full of gold, and others inhabited by naked cannibals. It was a fake which totally confused the English explorer.

What sort of creatures did Davis see on Baffin Island?

Davis wrote that he saw 'white bears of a monstrous bigness'. They were, of course, polar bears.

Who was Henry Hudson?

Hudson was an explorer who thought he had found the Northwest Passage in 1610, but it turned out to be Hudson Bay. He grew confused, his ship became trapped by ice, and his starving crew mutinied. Hudson, his son and a few followers were cast adrift in a small boat, and never seen again.

Henry Hudson and his followers in icy Hudson Bay.

Was Francis Drake a pirate?

Drake was known as the 'Queen's pirate', and he spent much of his life at sea attacking Spanish ships and stealing their treasure. He was not really a pirate but a 'privateer', because he was secretly carrying out the orders of Queen Elizabeth I. Spain was England's great rival at the time, and Elizabeth secretly encouraged Drake to make his pirate raids!

How did Drake earn his millions?

Drake captured a Spanish treasure ship called *Cacafuego*. When he returned to England, his ship was overflowing with *Cacafuego*'s cargo of gold, silver and magnificent jewels, with an estimated modern value of £25 million.

Francis Drake presents a coconut to Queen Elizabeth I.

What strange nut did Drake bring home?

A coconut! Drake presented a coconut to Queen Elizabeth, having discovered the delicious fruit during one of his voyages. The queen had a magnificent golden goblet made to hold the nut!

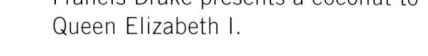

MAGELLAN'S MARVEL

Drake's was the second voyage to circle the globe. An expedition led by Portuguese explorer Ferdinand Magellan had completed a three-year voyage around the world in 1522. But only 18 of the 260 crew survived the voyage, and Magellan himself was not one of them.

Why did Drake chop off his friend's head?

Drake caught his friend Thomas Doughty plotting a mutiny. He put him on trial and found him guilty of mutiny and witchcraft. Drake had his friend's head cut off, and held it up, saying: 'This is the end of traitors!'

Why were spices so valuable?

Spices, such as pepper, cloves and nutmeg, could make explorers and adventurers very rich. They would sell them to Europeans who wanted the spices to disguise the terrible taste of rotten meat.

Did Drake live a humble life on his ship?

Drake liked to enjoy the finer things in life. While on board ship, he had his dinner served on silver dishes, while musicians played for him.

Why is Drake famous for playing bowls?

According to legend, Drake was playing bowls when the Spanish Armada attacked England in 1588. As it approached he said: 'We have time enough to finish the game and beat the Spaniards, too.' And he was right!

Where did Francis Drake travel in the *Golden Hind*?

When Drake sailed his ship, the *Golden Hind*, back into Plymouth on September 26, 1580, he completed one of the greatest voyages in history. He had sailed south and around the tip of South America, north along the west coast of America, then west across the Pacific and Indian Oceans, before rounding the southern tip of Africa and returning home. Drake and his crew had been at sea for almost three years, sailed over 86,000 kilometres and travelled right around the globe.

FOLDING BACK THE EARS

One of Magellan's sailors claimed to have heard of people in the East Indies who had ears so long that they used one for a mattress and the other for a blanket!

Who tried to buy a dragon's head?

After his piracy against their ships and the defeat of their Armada, Drake was not very popular with the Spanish. They called him 'The Dragon' and offered a reward of 20,000 ducats for his head!

Drake's ship, *Golden Hind*, during his epic voyage around the world.

Who lost a colony?

The English soldier, adventurer and poet Sir Walter Raleigh spent a fortune organising expeditions to try to start the first English colony in America. One group of settlers reached Roanoke Island in 1585, but had to be saved from starvation by Sir Francis Drake. A second group reached Roanoke in 1587, but within three years every trace of them had vanished. They became known as the Lost Colony, and their fate remains a mystery.

How much did John Cabot receive for his troubles?

Cabot was an Italian explorer who, in 1497, sailed west from Bristol in a ship called *Mathew* to find the treasures of the Indies for King Henry VII. He returned a month later, having in fact reached Newfoundland on the east coast of America. His reward from the king was £10!

Can Native Americans speak Welsh?

There is a legend in Wales of a Prince Madoc, who discovered a new land to the west in the twelfth century. He came home to gather shiploads of followers then sailed again for his New World. The myth was supported in the seventeenth century by the discovery of the Mandan tribe in North America, whose language is strangely similar to Welsh!

Did Raleigh invent pipe-smoking?

No, tobacco was widely smoked by the Native Americans. The Spanish introduced it to Europe, but Raleigh helped to make pipe-smoking fashionable in England. He even persuaded Queen Elizabeth I to try it!

How did Raleigh weigh smoke?

Raleigh once bet the queen that he could weigh the smoke from his pipe. He did so by weighing his tobacco, smoking it and then weighing the ashes from his pipe. He claimed the difference in the two weights must be the weight of the smoke.

John Cabot sets sail in *Mathew*.

What strange men did Raleigh write about?

Raleigh wrote that in Guiana he had found proof of the existence of 'men whose heads do grow beneath their shoulders'.

Did Raleigh really discover potatoes?

Potatoes were grown by the native people of South America. It was Spanish explorers who first brought them back to Europe, but Raleigh did help to introduce the new vegetable to England.

A MISSING CONTINENT

The Italian explorer Christopher Columbus discovered America in 1492 – by mistake. He thought the globe was smaller than it is, and believed he had sailed west as far as the Indies. In fact he had reached San Salvador in the Caribbean, and chanced upon an enormous, unknown continent. His discovery started a rush to explore this 'New World'.

Sir Walter Raleigh prepares to add the potato to the English diet.

How did Raleigh disappoint the King?

Raleigh sailed to South America at the age of 64, promising to find El Dorado for King James I. He returned empty-handed and the King ordered his head to be cut off.

What was El Dorado?

El Dorado was a mythical land of gold which European explorers believed they could find in South America. In 1585, Raleigh sailed up the Orinoco River in Venezuela, in search of its riches. He found no gold, but he did come across a strange food – the pineapple!

Who were the Pilgrim Fathers?

The Pilgrim Fathers were the 102 passengers (and two pet dogs) aboard *Mayflower*. They sailed across the Atlantic to start a new life in the New World of America. Leaving England on September 16, 1620, they landed 66 days later at a place they named Plymouth. Some of the Pilgrim Fathers were Puritans escaping from King James I's persecution of their religion. Others were just escaping from poverty.

Did anyone fall overboard?

One woman drowned, but a man who fell overboard was dragged back to safety with a boat-hook. Two babies were born during the voyage.

How did it smell on *Mayflower*?

Below deck, there was no ventilation and the ceiling was so low that you couldn't stand up. There was the stink of toilet buckets, vomit from the passengers' seasickness, stagnant water that lay in the bottom of the ship and the odour of the Pilgrims themselves – who were too modest to change their clothes.

The Pilgrim Fathers suffer below decks on the *Mayflower*.

What is Plymouth Rock?

It is the famous rock on which the Pilgrim Fathers first set foot when they stepped ashore. In 1774, the rock was dragged by oxen to stand in the town square, but it was taken back to the shore a century later.

A Native American painted in 1585 by a famous colonist named John White.

Did the same number of Pilgrims arrive in the New World?

Yes, but not the same ones! There were two deaths and two births during the voyage. A boy named Oceanus was born mid-Atlantic, and just as the New World was sighted a second boy was born. He was named Peregrine – and lived in America until he was 83!

Which Native American spoke English?

To the Pilgrims' amazement, they were welcomed to the New World by a Native American named Squanto who spoke good English. He had been kidnapped by slave-traders some years before and had learnt English before making his escape!

Was Plymouth the first colony?

No, a colony had already been established at Jamestown, Virginia. Its leader, the adventurer Captain John Smith, was famously saved from death when a 12-year-old Native American girl called Pocahontas begged her father, a local chief, to spare his life.

SHAKESPEARE'S SHIPWRECK

Sea Venture, a ship carrying colonists to Virginia in 1609, ran aground in Bermuda. William Shakespeare was inspired by the shipwreck and wrote his play *The Tempest*.

Were there cannibals in the New World?

Yes, but they were the colonists themselves! Some settlers in Jamestown were hopeless farmers, and had no idea how to trade with the local Native Americans. They became so hungry that they ended up eating each other!

Maori warriors dance during Cook's exploration of New Zealand.

What did the Maoris like to eat?

Cook noted that some Maoris he met at Queen Charlotte's Sound, New Zealand, were cannibals. They had recently captured and eaten a number of their enemies! Fortunately for Cook, the Maoris only wanted to trade with him.

Who was Captain Cook?

James Cook was the greatest explorer and navigator of the Pacific and Southern Oceans. Cook commanded three voyages and made so many discoveries that he completely changed the map of the globe. He sailed around the world twice, proved that New Zealand was made up of two islands, and claimed Australia for Britain. He also discovered several Pacific islands including Hawaii. Cook was welcomed to Hawaii as a god, but relations with the islanders grew less friendly. In 1779 a fight broke out in which Cook was stabbed to death.

Why did Cook give his sailors duffel bags?

Because his ships were packed with so many provisions there was no room for the sailors' traditional wooden chests. On Cook's first Pacific voyage, his ship *Endeavour*'s cargo included 450 kg of dried soup, 3,600 kg of pickled cabbage, 1,100 kg of raisins, 2,250 litres of vinegar, 5,450 litres of beer and 7,250 litres of brandy.

How did Cook prevent scurvy?

During long voyages, scurvy caused its victims' gums to bleed and their teeth to fall out, and they often died in agony. Cook believed fresh food prevented scurvy. He served up pickled cabbage and carrot marmalade, and kept live pigs, sheep and hens on board.

Which animal travelled around the world?

Cook had a goat on board one of his voyages to provide milk for the officers' coffee. It survived the voyage, just as it had survived a voyage around the world with a previous captain. It became the first goat in history to sail around the world twice!

How did Cook discover the Great Barrier Reef?

He discovered the gigantic reef only when *Endeavour* ran aground on it! The ship remained stuck for nearly a day, with water pouring in. Cook finally managed to refloat the boat, and the leak was patched with a sail covered in sheep dung.

TATTOOS

The fashion among sailors for decorating their bodies with tattoos began after Cook discovered the tattooed Pacific islanders on one of his voyages.

What did Cook's men see bouncing along the Australian coast?

They saw a creature like a wild dog, which jumped like a hare when it ran, and could travel faster than a greyhound. One of Cook's crew noted that the native Aborigines called the animal a 'kangaru'.

What happened to Cook's body?

Cook's third voyage ended in tragedy when he was killed in Hawaii. The Hawaiians cut up his body and burnt his flesh. Then they returned his bones to Cook's comrades, who buried them at sea.

Traveller's Tales

Two of the greatest books of adventure were popular in Cook's time. Jonathan Swift's *Gulliver's Travels* (1726) told of the fantastic travels of a ship's surgeon in the Pacific. Daniel Defoe's *Robinson Crusoe* (1719) was based on the real story of a shipwrecked Scottish sailor.

Endeavour runs aground on Australia's Great Barrier Reef.

Burke and Wills with one of their trusty camels.

Who were Burke and Wills?

In 1861, Robert O'Hara Burke, an Irish police superintendent, and William John Wills, an English surveyor, became the first explorers to cross Australia. They travelled from the south to the north coast, but did not survive the return journey. The explorers made it back to their supply camp at Cooper's Creek, only to find a note saying their support team had left a few hours earlier – with all the fresh camels! The two explorers had been abandoned to die of exhaustion and starvation.

What did Burke and Wills travel on?

Twenty-four camels were imported to help carry Burke and Wills and their baggage! When the party left Melbourne, people were amazed – they had never seen these humped beasts before.

Did camels live in Australia?

No, but they do now! Many expeditions after Burke's used camels to carry their equipment. Stray camels bred in the wild, and there are now some 15,000 roaming the Australian deserts!

What did Burke and Wills' camels get to drink?

Burke's camels were loaded down with scientific and medical equipment, guns and rockets, tents and camp-beds, and mirrors and beads to trade with Aborigines. Among the provisions were 270 litres of rum – for the camels to drink!

TASTY GRUB

One of Burke's biggest mistakes was that he didn't ask the Australian Aborigines for help. They were experts at finding food in the barren deserts – including the tasty, fat larvae of beetles, called witchetty grubs.

Were conditions good at the Cooper's Creek camp?

No! It was so hot that a thermometer in the shade exploded! The explorers had to hang their stores from trees because of a plague of rats, and there were swarms of flies and mosquitoes.

Was Burke a keen reader?

He must have been. He threw away his heavy medical equipment early on, but took dozens of books all the way to the north coast to help him pass the time!

Was there much food in the outback?

Burke and Wills found rats, crows, snakes and seeds to add to their supplies. John McDouall Stuart, another explorer, ate thistles and mice!

Who was stopped by fire?

The Scottish explorer John McDouall Stuart attempted to cross Australia at the same time as Burke and Wills. He turned back when hostile Aborigines set fire to the bush in front of him.

Which explorer was an underground writer?

Charles Sturt, an English army officer, explored the Australian interior in 1844. He found that the climate was so hot that he had to write his diary in an underground chamber to stop the ink evaporating!

GETTING IN TOUCH

John McDouall Stuart succeeded in crossing Australia from south to north at his third attempt. He made the return trip safely, and his route was used to lay a telegraph wire across Australia.

Who was John King?

A rescue party sent to find Burke and Wills met a group of Aborigines. Among them was a half-mad, starving man in rags. He was so sunburnt and filthy, they thought he was a dark-skinned Aborigine. However, he was John King, the last survivor of Burke and Wills' party.

Aborigines hunted in the Australian outback with spears and boomerangs.

How many languages did Burton and Speke speak?

Sir Richard Burton and John Hanning Speke set out from Zanzibar in 1857 to find the source of the Nile. Burton spoke over 25 languages, could use sign language, and once kept an army of trained monkeys – each with a rank and title – so that he could learn how to imitate them!

What did Burton and Speke take with them?

Their equipment included pickles, cigars, snuff, 60 kg of gunpowder, a table and two chairs, pillows, silverware, pens, paper, sealing wax, an artist's kit, 30 kg of nails, four umbrellas, 2,000 fish-hooks, 24 penknives and a Union Jack.

Sir Richard Burton with an army of bearers carrying his equipment.

FAMOUS CLAMS

A part of Lake Victoria is known today as Speke Gulf. Burton left his mark on a smaller discovery – a freshwater clam from Lake Tanganyika is known as *Grandidiera burtoni*.

Why did people search for the source of the Nile?

Africa was known in Britain as the 'Dark Continent' because even by 1800 it remained a land of danger and mystery. The River Nile had been the centre of ancient Egyptian society, and a map drawn by the ancient geographer Ptolemy showed the river flowing from two great lakes. For modern explorers, the source of the Nile became the ultimate goal at the heart of the Dark Continent.

Who discovered the secret of eternal life?

The secret to eternal life was said to have been discovered by a character called Prester John. He was a shadowy, mythical figure who was rumoured to rule over a Christian kingdom of incredible wealth in the heart of Africa.

Which explorer did a striptease?

In 1770, Scottish explorer James Bruce of Kinnaird searched for the source of the Nile. He was forced to strip for the King of Sennar's harem so that the women could admire his white skin!

Why did Speke's ear whistle?

John Hanning Speke makes sketches of Africa's amazing wildlife.

When a beetle started burrowing into his eardrum, Speke tried to remove it with a penknife. This not only made him deaf, but created a hole between his nose and ear, which made a loud whistle every time he blew his nose!

Who did Burton try to kidnap?

Burton was an eccentric and flamboyant Englishman who had studied languages at Oxford University. He once tried to kidnap a beautiful nun. However, he was horrified to find that, in the dark, he had abducted her ugly prioress by mistake!

Did Burton and Speke stay healthy?

No, both explorers were so weakened by fever that they had to be carried in hammocks by their African porters. Speke became blind from an eye condition, and when the explorers discovered Lake Tanganyika – the longest freshwater lake in the world – he couldn't see it!

Who did Speke discover on the banks of the Nile?

To his amazement, Speke met the eccentric English explorer Samuel Baker, who was investigating the River Nile with his wife Florence!

What did Speke measure in the kingdom of Buganda?

When Speke made a second journey to Lake Victoria, he visited the kingdom of Buganda – where he carefully recorded the body measurements of the women in the royal family!

SAMUEL AND FLORENCE BAKER

Samuel Baker met his wife Florence in Bulgaria, before setting off with her to search for the River Nile's source! He nearly lost her to a native chief who wanted to swap her for one of his own wives! Florence told the chief, in no uncertain terms, that this was not an option. There was also a third member of the Bakers' party – a monkey named Wallady.

What caused Burton and Speke's famous argument?

After the explorers had discovered Lake Tanganyika, Speke travelled on alone to Lake Victoria. He guessed, correctly, that this was the source of the Nile, but Burton argued that the true source was his lake – Tanganyika. Speke died in a mysterious shooting accident shortly before the two explorers were due to debate the issue.

How did Mungo Park lose his clothes?

During an expedition to explore the River Niger in 1796, Scottish doctor Mungo Park was set upon by bandits, who stole his horse, weapons and clothes. He was left naked and alone, surrounded by hostile tribes and ferocious beasts, hundreds of kilometres from the nearest settlement.

Who were Livingstone and Stanley?

Dr David Livingstone was the most famous Victorian explorer of Africa. He worked in a Scottish cotton mill from the age of ten, but later travelled to Africa as a missionary wishing to stop the slave trade. He became the first European to cross Africa from coast to coast, and discovered Victoria Falls. Henry Morton Stanley was a journalist told by the *New York Herald* to 'Find Livingstone!' after the explorer had disappeared on his third expedition. Stanley not only found Livingstone, but himself became a famous explorer.

'Dr Livingstone, I presume.'

Did Livingstone have any problems with lions?

Yes, he once saw a woman devoured by one, and was himself badly mauled. The lion seized hold of his left arm and shook him like a rag-doll. He was rescued by his African companions, but had to set the shattered bones of his arm without anaesthetic.

How about hippos and crocodiles?

Livingstone was once flung into a crocodile-infested river when his boat was capsized by a large female hippo.

Did Livingstone convert many Africans?

No, he was a better explorer than missionary. He only managed to convert one local chief, named Sechele, to Christianity – but the chief still didn't want to give up his five wives!

How did African women make a point?

Livingstone was alarmed when some African women he met smiled to reveal their teeth – which had been filed down to sharp points!

What was 'Livingstone's Rouser'?

The 'Rouser' was a home-made pill Livingstone took regularly to try to combat malaria and dysentery, two diseases which plagued adventurers in Africa. Even so, he had constant attacks of fever which often left him so weak that he had to be carried.

Natives use fishing nets to snare Henry Stanley's boat, the *Lady Alice*.

Was Stanley American?

Stanley was actually born in Wales. He was abandoned at a workhouse at the age of six, ran away to sea and then settled in America. He fought in the American Civil War, then became a journalist writing reports of battles between the army and Native Americans.

What are the most famous words in the history of exploration?

'Dr Livingstone, I presume.' This was what Stanley said to the frail white man he approached on November 10, 1871, at Ujiji on the banks of Lake Tanganyika. Stanley was the first European that Livingstone had seen in six years.

What happened to Livingstone's body?

Livingstone refused to return home with Stanley, and died from fever in 1873. His heart was buried in Africa. His body was carried by his loyal African companions on a nine-month journey to the coast, taken to England and finally buried in Westminster Abbey, London.

Who caught Stanley in a net?

Stanley completed Livingstone's work by navigating rivers in a portable boat called *Lady Alice*. He was frequently attacked by hostile natives, and one group stretched fishing nets across the river to trap his boat before launching a hail of poisoned arrows.

How did Stanley travel through Africa?

His vast caravan of followers must have been one of the most extraordinary sights ever seen in Africa. It rumbled through the country with 353 African porters, as well as the 700 followers and slaves of the Arab slave-trader Tippu Tib.

A WOMAN'S PLACE

Mary Kingsley, a London lady, shocked Victorian society by travelling alone to Africa to collect specimens of unknown fish. She shared meals with cannibals, was thrown from capsized canoes, and once slapped a crocodile on the snout with an oar to stop it climbing into her boat!

Why was it dangerous to explore Arabia?

Arabia, on the south-west corner of Asia, was home to Muslim tribes who would attack, torture and kill Christian travellers. It was also forbidden, and very dangerous, for Christians to enter the Arabian holy cities of Mecca and Medina.

Lawrence of Arabia rode into battles and adventures on the back of a camel.

Who was Lawrence of Arabia?

T.E. Lawrence was a British officer in Arabia during the First World War. There, he found himself charging into battle on the back of a camel, leading Arab forces in raids against the Turks. His incredible adventures in this part of the world led him to become known as Lawrence of Arabia. He published a famous book about his exploits called the *Seven Pillars of Wisdom*, before dying in a motorcycling accident.

What did Lawrence wear?

Lawrence dressed in the costume of a rich Arab. He wore a headdress and flowing robes of pure white silk, and kept a huge, curved dagger of gold tucked in his belt.

Which woman amazed the Arabs?

The archaeologist Gertrude Bell explored the Arabian deserts before the First World War, calmly greeting Arab tribes who had never seen a European before – let alone a European woman.

Who made a hole in his camel?

Lawrence had a whole stable of racing camels, and was once seen mounting a camel at full gallop by seizing its tail and hauling himself into the saddle. But during one fierce battle, he mistakenly shot his own camel through the skull!

ARABIAN NIGHTS

Sir Richard Burton is also famous for his translation into English of *The Arabian Nights*, a collection of Arabic folk-tales. But the explorer couldn't help but embellish the stories slightly by adding details from his own adventures.

Who refused to travel in disguise?

Charles Doughty wandered among the Muslim people of Arabia for two years from 1876. He was a large, clumsy man with an enormous red beard, who refused to disguise the fact that he was a Christian gentleman. Somehow, he survived to write of his travels.

Who bathed in urine?

Doughty was taken in by generous Bedouin tribes and shared their food, which included dates, roast locusts, camel and hedgehog. When Doughty used precious drinking water to wash with, the Bedouin were horrified – they used camel urine!

How did Doughty's magic get him into trouble?

When Doughty wrote notes and made sketches in his diary, the Arabs thought he was weaving magic spells. They abandoned the red-haired non-believer in the scorching desert, and he was stoned, beaten, stripped and robbed.

Who was W.G. Palgrave?

Palgrave was one of the most mysterious adventurers, and he crossed Arabia in 1862. He was an Oxford scholar, a priest whose missionary work was blessed by the Pope, and a spy working for Napoleon III. He also disguised himself as a Syrian doctor!

Were Burton's many disguises successful?

Yes, he always travelled undetected, and was even given work as a doctor. In Cairo, Egypt, at the beginning of his pilgrimage, he used hypnosis to cure a slave-girl of snoring!

Sir Richard Burton in Arabia, wearing one of his many disguises.

Who liked to travel in disguise?

Sir Richard Burton, who explored Africa with Speke, disguised himself as a Muslim doctor by the name of Abdullah when he travelled across Arabia. He stained his skin with henna, grew a beard, mastered Persian and Arabic – and in 1853 he even entered the forbidden cities of Medina and Mecca.

Who vanished in the Arctic?

The famous explorer Sir John Franklin led an Arctic expedition to search for the Northwest Passage in 1845. He sailed with 134 men in the steamships *Terror* and *Erebus*. In Greek myth Erebus is the road to hell. The ships were well-named – the explorer was never seen alive again. For 14 years the whole country wondered about Franklin's fate and several rescue expeditions searched the Arctic for him.

Balloons carry messages across the Arctic in the search for John Franklin.

Why did rescuers release balloons?

Rescuers sent up balloons with messages for Franklin attached to long fuses. As the balloons drifted over the Arctic and the fuses burnt shorter, the messages fluttered down on to the ice.

How was Franklin's fate revealed?

Rescuers met Inuit people who carried silver forks and spoons from Franklin's ships and said they had seen starving white men staggering across the ice. At last, a pile of stones was found containing Franklin's body and a note revealing the explorer's fate. Beyond it lay a trail of skeletons.

THE CROW'S NEST

The crow's nest was invented by Captain William Scoresby Sr, for use in the Arctic. Originally, it was a barrel strapped to the top of a ship's mast that was protected by an umbrella of canvas. From the crow's nest, a lookout could use a telescope to search for a route through the ice.

Who became stranded in the Antarctic?

What had happened to Franklin?

His ships had become stuck in the ice, and his party spent two winters trapped on board. Every last one of them had died of starvation, exhaustion and disease as they finally tried to walk across the ice to safety.

Who became cannibals?

The last survivors of Franklin's party became so desperate that they took to eating the bodies of their dead companions.

How did a spirit guide Franklin's rescuers?

Franklin's wife gave rescuers a map which had been revealed during a seance by the spirit of a four-year-old girl who had died in Ireland. The map was later shown to have pinpointed the exact spot where Franklin died!

What methods of transport did Ernest Shackleton use?

In 1909 the Irish explorer Ernest Shackleton walked to within 156 kilometres of the South Pole. His expedition ended up dragging their sledges themselves, having tried dogs, ponies and even a motor car!

Ernest Shackleton reaches South Georgia during the epic rescue of his expedition.

When Shackleton and twenty-eight men who had answered his advert attempted to cross Antarctica in 1914, his ship *Endurance* became trapped in ice for 282 days. The ice then crushed the ship, and Shackleton's party were stranded for 165 days on icebergs, which rocked so much they became seasick!

How did Shackleton rescue his party?

Shackleton made a 1,000-kilometre voyage in a 7-metre lifeboat through the world's roughest and iciest seas to reach the island of South Georgia. He even had to survive a hurricane which sunk a 508-tonne steamer! The explorer then marched over a mountain that had never before been climbed, found help and went on to rescue every one of his men.

What did Shackleton's stranded party eat?

Their menu included seal and penguin meat, seal-bone soup, limpets and seaweed.

How did Shackleton advertise for people to explore with him?

'Men wanted for Hazardous Journey. Small wages, bitter cold, long months of complete darkness, constant danger, safe return doubtful. Honour and recognition in case of success.'

Why did Shackleton's men wish they had an umbrella?

Because, as the ice broke up enough to allow them to launch their lifeboats towards nearby Elephant Island, a flock of birds bombarded them with droppings!

Scott and his men haul their supplies
and equipment to the Pole on sledges.

Who was Captain Scott?

Robert Falcon Scott was a British naval officer who set out on skis across the icy wastes of Antarctica, aiming to become the first human to stand at the very bottom of the world, the South Pole. Scott reached the Pole with four companions on January 17, 1912, only to find he had been beaten to his goal by the Norwegian explorer Roald Amundsen.

DOG CUTLETS

Amundsen used 52 Inuit dogs to pull his supplies on sledges. When he reached a place he named 'Butchers', he slaughtered the weakest dogs for food. He later wrote: 'We treated ourselves to dog cutlets... It was excellent.'

What did Scott find at the South Pole?

Scott found the tracks of Amundsen's dogs, and a Norwegian flag fluttering in the wind. Amundsen had also left behind a little tent, containing some letters with a note asking Scott to pass them on to the Norwegian king. There were also some mittens, and a spare navigational instrument so that Scott could measure the exact location of his defeat. Scott wrote of the Pole: 'Great God! This is an awful place.'

What did Scott's party eat at Christmas, 1911?

Their Christmas dinner consisted of horsemeat with onion and curry powder, ground biscuit, plum pudding, cocoa with raisins, and a dessert of caramel and crystallised ginger.

How did Scott and his party stay warm?

In the early days of the twentieth century, before the invention of modern materials, Antarctic explorers wore many layers of clothing. This would include thick underwear, two flannel shirts, a jersey, a sweater, cloth trousers, a jacket, an outer suit, a balaclava and woollen mittens beneath enormous fur mitts. Their boots and sleeping bags were made from reindeer fur.

How did Scott's party transport their supplies?

They had no dogs, so they dragged their supplies behind them on sledges. By the time of Scott's death, the load the explorers were hauling along included 15 kilograms of fossils that they had collected on their journey to the Pole!

Who said: 'I am just going outside, I may be some time.'

These were the last words of one of Scott's party, Captain Oates, who suffered terrible frostbite during the return journey. Afraid of slowing his companions down, he left their tent during a blizzard and walked to his death.

How do we know about Scott's journey?

The explorers' bodies were found eight months later, along with film showing the dejected group at the Pole. Scott had his diary tucked under his arm. The last entry, March 29, 1912, reads: 'The end cannot be far. It seems a pity but I do not think I can write more.'

How far did Scott's party walk?

They tramped through the snow for 2,500 kilometres – that's five times the distance from London to Edinburgh! When Scott and his two surviving comrades died, trapped in their tent by blizzards, they were less than 20 kilometres from the safety of their next food store.

Scott and his party at the South Pole on January 17, 1912.

Oates

Scott

Evans

Bowers

Wilson

Who first stood on top of the world?

Sherpa Tensing Norkey standing 'on top of the world'.

At 11.30 am, on May 29, 1953, the mountaineers Edmund Hillary (a New Zealander) and Tensing Norkey (a guide from the Sherpa people of Nepal) became the first explorers to stand on the top of Mount Everest, the world's highest mountain. They were part of a British expedition led by Colonel John Hunt. News of their incredible achievement reached Britain on the day of Queen Elizabeth II's coronation.

Were they really the first ones to the top?

Probably, but 30 years earlier, in 1924, the mountaineer George Mallory climbed away from his support team and disappeared into a veil of mist only a few hundred metres from Everest's summit. He was never seen alive again.

What was Hillary's profession?

He was a beekeeper, and he did not become a mountaineer until he was 26 years old.

What did Hillary and Tensing bury at Everest's peak?

They spent 15 minutes on the roof of the world. Hillary buried a small crucifix that Hunt had given to him, while Tensing buried a pencil, a toy cat made out of black cloth and sweets as offerings to the mountain's gods.

Why aren't Charles Evans and Tom Bourdillon famous?

Evans and Bourdillon were the first of Hunt's party to attempt the final ascent of Everest. Only after they had turned back because they were short of oxygen did Hillary and Tensing begin their own climb.

What did Hillary and Tensing eat before their final ascent?

They had a meal of apricots and sardines. The temperature in their tent as they ate was an unbelievable –27°C!

ENGLISH AIR

Early mountaineers climbed in old-fashioned tweed clothes and boots without spikes. At first, they did not even have oxygen to help them breathe. Mallory felt the use of oxygen was 'unsporting', but both he and Hillary used it. Sherpa guides laughed at the heavy bottles containing what they called 'English Air'.

Did Mallory reach the summit?

Nobody knows! Mallory's body, dressed in tweed clothes and perfectly preserved by the cold, was not found for another 75 years! His camera was missing, so we can't be sure if he died on the way up or back down.

How did Edward Whymper nearly die in the Alps?

In 1865, Edward Whymper achieved one of the first great feats of mountaineering by climbing the Matterhorn, a treacherous mountain in the Alps. On the descent, four of his comrades fell to their death. The rope attaching them to Whymper snapped – saving his life.

Which clergyman climbed the highest mountain in North America?

Hudson Stuck conquered Mount McKinley in 1913. He was a vicar from England who preached in Alaska, where his job-title was Archdeacon of the Yukon!

What famous phrase did Mallory invent?

When asked why he wished to climb Everest, Mallory answered: 'Because it's there.'

George Mallory and his comrade Andrew Irvine tackle Mount Everest with the most basic of equipment.

According to his friends, Sir Malcolm Campbell visited a fortune-teller before each of his record attempts. Despite what Campbell called a 'ticklish moment' when a tyre burst on *Bluebird* at 290 mph (467 km/h), the fortune-teller seems to have always had good news for him.

Whose body was never found?

Donald Campbell died in January 1967 trying to become the first man to travel across water at over 300 mph (483 km/h), when his *Bluebird* boat somersaulted on Coniston Water. Campbell's teddy bear mascot was found, but the boat and his remains were not recovered for over 30 years.

Donald Campbell with the record-breaking car *Bluebird*.

Which father and son were the speed kings?

In the twentieth century, British adventurers explored physical barriers as well as geographical ones. Sir Malcolm Campbell and his son Donald used their famous *Bluebird* cars and boats to shatter world speed records on land and water. Through the 1920s and '30s, Malcolm became the first human to travel over land at 200 mph (322 km/h), and then at 300 mph (483 km/h). In the 1950s and '60s, Donald took up the challenge, and pushed up the record to an amazing 400 mph (644 km/h).

Which explorer went looking for locusts?

The modern explorer Wilfred Thesiger travelled to the mysterious Arabian desert, known as the Empty Quarter, as part of a locust research expedition in 1945. He became the first European to see the treacherous quicksands of Umm al Sammim.

When did a team of women walk to the South Pole?

On January 24, 2000, British women Caroline Hamilton, Ann Daniels, Pom Oliver, Rosie Stancer and Zoe Hudson became the first all-female team to walk to the South Pole – in temperatures as low as –50 °C.

Why didn't Sir Francis Chichester dress for dinner?

In 1960, Chichester made the fastest ever solo Atlantic crossing in his yacht *Gipsy Moth III*. He had planned to wear a dinner jacket each evening, but changed his mind when the jacket went mouldy!

How old was Chichester when he circled the globe?

Chichester completed a 45,000-kilometre voyage around the world in May 1967, at the age of 65. He spent 119 days at sea in *Gipsy Moth IV*.

Amy Johnson with her aeroplane *Jason*.

Who first crossed Antarctica?

Dr Vivian Fuchs led an expedition across the frozen continent in 1957 – 40 years after Shackleton's failed attempt. Fuchs had the distinct advantage of travelling in tracked motor vehicles called sno-cats, and having an aeroplane to drop supplies!

How did Amy Johnson fix her wings?

Johnson, who was the daughter of a fish merchant from Hull, patched up the wings of her battered aeroplane by using sticking plasters.

Who is Sir Ranulph Twisleton-Wykeham Fiennes?

Fiennes is an English adventurer who in 1992–3, with Michael Stroud, made the first unsupported crossing of Antarctica. They overcame frostbite and foot infections, and dragged behind them sledges weighing 220 kg (the weight of four or five people!).

Why did Amy Johnson learn martial arts?

In 1930, Amy Johnson in her second-hand aeroplane *Jason* became the first woman to fly solo from England to Australia. She had trained in the martial art of ju-jitsu to fight off the unwelcome attentions of Arab sheikhs when she stopped to refuel!

INFINITY AND BEYOND!

Now that explorers and adventurers have filled in most of the gaps on the maps of the world, they have to look to space for a new challenge. In 1991, Helen Sharman became the first British astronaut in space, and four years later Michael Foale became the first Briton to make a spacewalk.

Index

I

J

K

L